FOOTPATHS FOR FITNESS

BERKSHIRE

FOOTPATHS FOR FITNESS
BERKSHIRE

Nick Channer

COUNTRYSIDE BOOKS

NEWBURY BERKSHIRE

First published 2008
© Nick Channer, 2008

COUNTRYSIDE BOOKS
3 Catherine Road
Newbury, Berkshire

To view our complete range of books,
please visit us at
www.countrysidebooks.co.uk

ISBN 978 1 84674 088 6

Maps by Gelder Design & Mapping
Photographs by the author
Cover photograph by David Weller

Designed by Peter Davies, Nautilus Design
Produced through MRM Associates Ltd., Reading
Printed by Information Press, Oxford

*All material for the manufacture of this book was
sourced from sustainable forests.*

CONTENTS

**FOOTPATHS
FOR FITNESS**

FOOTPATHS FOR FITNESS

FOOTPATHS FOR FITNESS — GRADE 3 – HIKE

Introduction

According to recent government guidelines, every adult and child should exercise five times a week to halve their prospects of developing a chronic disease. One hour of exercise per day is normally enough to stop obesity and other life-threatening conditions.

So what measures can be taken to banish poor health, congested arteries and an expanding waistline? Well, there's the gym, of course, then there's swimming and jogging and cycling and various other quite strenuous activities. However, what many people often overlook – even though it is the most obvious form of exercise – is the simple pleasure of country walking to help keep fit and healthy.

With 140,000 miles of public rights of way in England and Wales alone – and many of those footpaths are in the Home Counties of the south – who needs a gymnasium to improve your fitness levels? Walking has everything – the chance to keep fit at a pace to suit yourself, classic scenery providing the perfect rural backdrop, often ideal weather conditions, magnificent views and a chance to learn about the natural and man-made history of our landscape.

The 20 walks included in this guide fit those criteria perfectly but, most important of all, they offer the chance to exercise in the great outdoors. The walks are all graded – starting with short, easy routes for beginners, then progressing to middle-ranking, medium length walks for those with a little more experience. The final three circuits are the longest and convey a hint of adventure. These can be attempted by novice walkers or those who have been overcoming health problems when they have attained a suitable level of fitness – in other words a goal to work towards.

But there is more to a good walk than simply putting one foot in front of the other and savouring the scenery. Take a good map with you to help navigate your way round the route; the Ordnance Survey Explorer series is the best for walking. Don't leave home without a small rucksack for carrying a camera, a pair of binoculars for studying wildlife, an adequate supply of bottled water and a small snack, including, perhaps, some chocolate or fruit. Most importantly take a waterproof jacket, a woolly hat and a fleece in winter. A sturdy pair of shoes or boots is also essential.

Happy walking!

N. Channw

PUBLISHER'S NOTE

We hope that you obtain considerable enjoyment from this book; great care has been taken in its preparation. Although at the time of publication all routes followed public rights of way or permitted paths, diversion orders can be made and permissions withdrawn.

We cannot, of course, be held responsible for such diversion orders and any inaccuracies in the text which result from these or any other changes to the routes nor any damage which might result from walkers trespassing on private property. We are anxious though that all details covering the walks are kept up to date and would therefore welcome information from readers which would be relevant to future editions.

The simple sketch maps that accompany the walks in this book are based on notes made by the author whilst checking out the routes on the ground. They are designed to show you how to reach the start, to point out the main features of the overall circuit and they contain a progression of numbers that relate to the paragraphs of the text.

However, for the benefit of a proper map, we do recommend that you purchase the relevant Ordnance Survey sheet covering your walk. The Ordnance Survey maps are widely available, especially through booksellers and local newsagents.

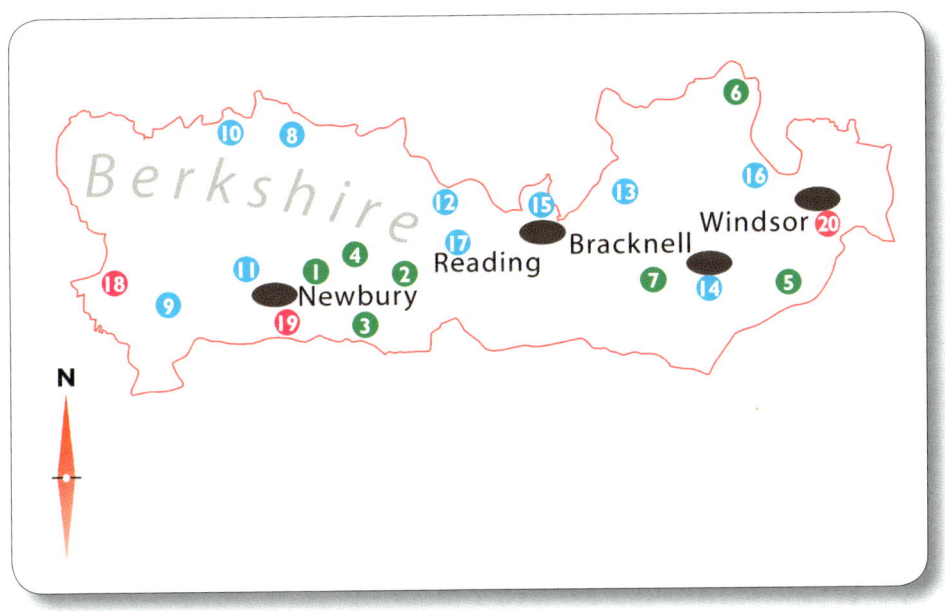

Area map showing location of the walks

1 Cold Ash
Woodland Clearings and Tranquil Paths

■ *Gentle countryside to start you on your way.* ■

GRADE: 1
ESTIMATED CALORIE BURN: 500

Distance: 3 miles
Stiles: None
Time: 1½ – 2 hours
Map: OS Explorer 158 Newbury and Hungerford.
Starting point: The free car park at the village hall in Cold Ash.
GR 509703
How to get there: From the A4 at Thatcham head west towards
Newbury. Turn right into Northfield Road at the traffic lights and follow
it towards Cold Ash. Head uphill, passing the Castle pub on the right
and the church on the left. Turn left just beyond the crossroads into the
free car park at the village hall bordering the recreation ground.
Refreshments: The Castle at Cold Ash is a traditional, unspoilt village
pub situated close to the walk's start and finish point.
Telephone: 01635 863232.

This is an easy walk to tackle, with only a couple of undemanding
ascents – ideal for a bright winter morning or an early evening in summer.
This, I think, is one of Berkshire's prettiest walks – one reason among many
to try it. Starting in the centre of Cold Ash, the walk soon heads for gently
undulating farmland and then into dense woodland, providing welcome
shade from the sun. This middle, leafy section is one of the walk's highlights.
Here, on a perfect summer's day you can enjoy the peace and tranquillity of
the setting and savour the natural beauty of the woodland clearings. With
a little physical effort but enough exertion to work up an appetite, by the
time you reach Bucklebury Alley and the closing stages of the walk, you
should feel the benefits of this memorable ramble.

1 From the car park turn right and follow the road down to the **Castle pub**
on the left. Turn left at this point, keeping the inn on your left, and follow
Gladstone Lane to the next junction. Go straight over to join a bridleway
and follow it between clumps of holly trees. Pass a pretty thatched cottage
on the left and continue between trees and hedgerows. Opposite you at
the next junction is a gateway leading to a small private graveyard where
nuns from the nearby convent are buried. Turn left, beneath some beech
trees, and walk up the track to the road. Turn right and pass the entrance
to **St Gabriel's Convent**. For many years the nuns here were engaged in
farming their own land and could regularly be seen ploughing the fields

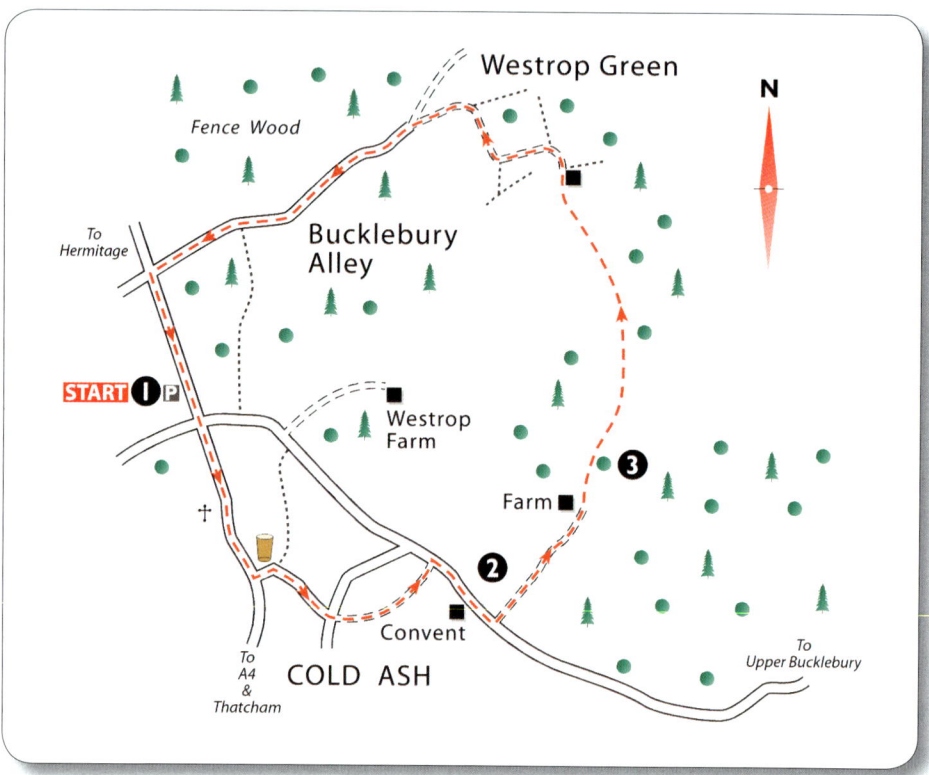

by tractor, their distinctive habits billowing in the breeze. Pass the Roman Catholic church and primary school and continue along the road. On the opposite side are rows of houses and bungalows. Keep going until you come to a bridleway on the left running down by a property called **Holly Slade**.

2 Take the track and follow it over a cattle grid. There are delightful views over rolling fields enclosed by trees. Walk towards a bungalow and ahead of you are superb views across the **Pang valley**. Veer left just before the bungalow and pass beside farm outbuildings to a gate. Aim half right in the field and make for a galvanised gate on the far side, leading into woodland. After a few paces, turn left along the tree-lined path.

3 Follow the path and, at length, you reach several cottages. Keep left here along a track, avoiding a path on the right. Turn left at the next main T-junction and follow the lane through **Westrop Wood**, rising gently to

■ *The Castle Inn at Cold Ash.* ■

reach some houses and bungalows. Beyond them are several picturesque cottages, including **Cherry Cottage** which is thatched. Pass **The White House** and **Drove Lane** on the right and the entrance to **Pine Lodge** on the left. Continue along the road to the next main junction, turn left and return to the car park where the walk began.

■ *Douai Abbey.* ■

This gently undulating walk offers a fine mix of field and woodland paths linking the village of Beenham with the magnificent buildings of Douai Abbey. For many years, until its closure in the late 1990s, this was a well-respected Roman Catholic public school, noted for its striking architectural features. After they were expelled from their monastery at Douai in northern France on anti-clerical grounds, an order of Benedictine monks fled across the English Channel to Berkshire, settling in the English countryside near Beenham to the west of Reading. Some sections can be wet and muddy in winter but the walk is one to enjoy whatever the season and an ideal circular ramble for anyone new to walking.

GRADE: 1
ESTIMATED CALORIE BURN: 510

Distance: 3 miles
Stiles: 4
Time: 1½ – 2 hours
Map: OS Explorer 159 Reading, Wokingham and Pangbourne.
Starting point: The Six Bells pub in Beenham. GR 586688
How to get there: From Newbury or Reading follow the A4. Between Theale and Woolhampton you will see signs for the village of Beenham to the north of the main road. Take the road, follow it to the village and beyond the centre on the right is the Six Bells pub and car park. Please check with the landlord before leaving your vehicle here while doing the walk. If the pub is especially busy you may be asked to park elsewhere in the village.
Refreshments: The Six Bells is a recently refurbished village inn offering fine dining, real ales and bar food. Telephone: 0118 971 3368.

---

1 From the car park turn left and follow the road briefly to the junction with **Clay Lane** which you follow as it bends left. Keep ahead at the byway sign and turn right at the first footpath. Follow the enclosed path into dense woodland, veer right at the fork and, on breaking cover from the trees, branch left along the bridleway towards the buildings of **Douai Abbey**. Soon you reach wooden fencing before crossing over a drive leading to houses. Follow the path to the road and turn right, crossing the junction with Abbey Gardens. Keep right at the junction just beyond it, following the road for **Bucklebury**. Pass the buildings of Douai and continue along the road, passing the main car park. On the left along here is **Croft Cottage**, with several farm outbuildings seen just beyond. Avoid a track just before them on the right and keep ahead between high hedgerows. Soon a footpath crosses the route and just beyond this point the road bends left.

2 Take the footpath on the right on the bend and follow it across the middle of a field towards outbuildings at **Copyhold Farm**. On reaching them, cross a stile by a galvanised gate and turn left along a track. As it bends left go forward over a stile by a sign: 'Please keep dogs on lead'. Go diagonally across the field, keeping to the right of a housing estate beyond it. There are two stiles in the field corner, one half hidden by trees, the other in the fence a few paces to the right. Head for the latter, cross over and turn immediately right.

■ *Picturesque cottages passed on the walk.* ■

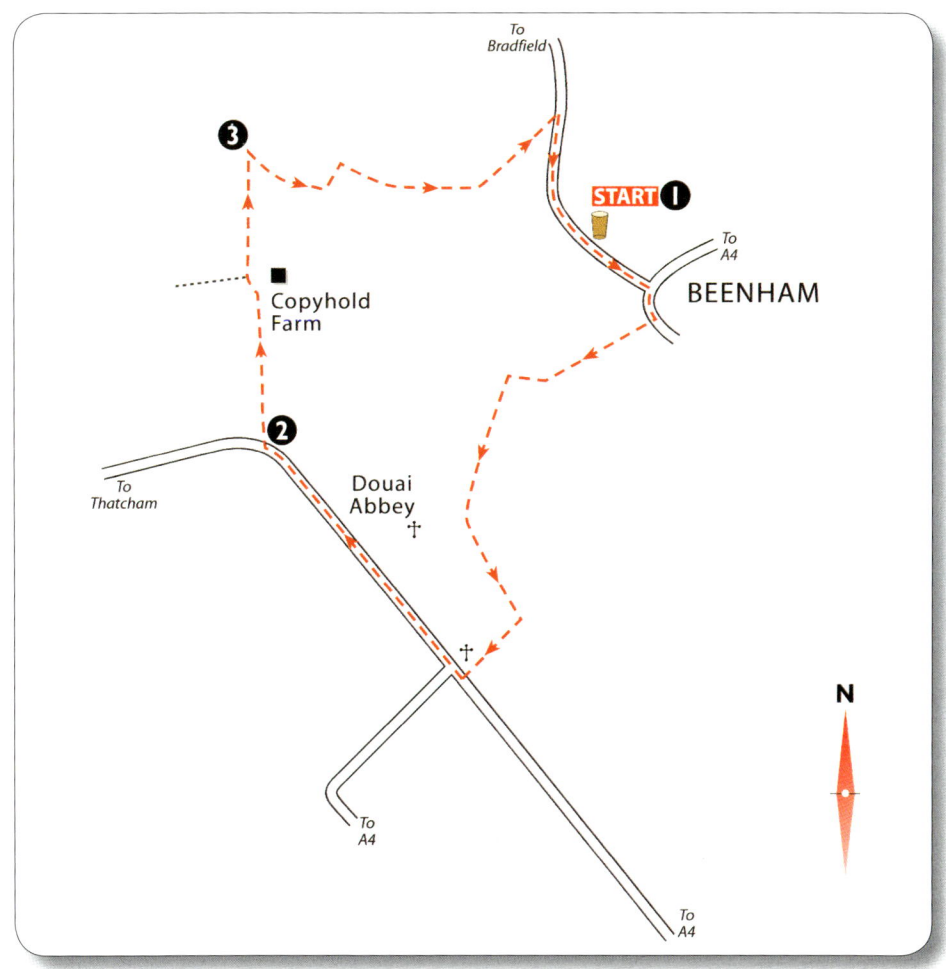

3 Follow the field perimeter, swing left in the corner and make for a stile providing access into woodland. Follow the obvious path through the trees and along a boardwalk. Cross several streams and when the path forks, keep right. Pass beside an electricity substation nestling among the trees and at the next path junction, by a sign for **Greyfield Wood**, turn left. Follow the track as it swings right to the road and turn right. Return to the pub car park which will be found on the left as you enter **Beenham**.

3 *Brimpton*
On the Level

■ *Showing the way.* ■

There are **no steep hills or** dramatic ascents on this delightful walk, much of which is beside the meandering Enborne – one of my favourite rivers in the region. Rising on the Berkshire/Hampshire border to the south of Newbury, it journeys quietly and without fuss to meet the Kennet at nearby Woolhampton. Keep an eye out for wildlife on the walk, you might spot a heron in the watery reaches. The spire of Brimpton church is seen at intervals throughout the walk, acting as a welcome and reassuring landmark. You'll enjoy the undemanding meadow stretches and, for novice walkers, the last leg over open ground towards Brimpton church is a great way to round off the ramble.

GRADE : 1
ESTIMATED CALORIE BURN: 490

Distance: 3 miles
Stiles: None
Time: 1½ – 2 hours
Map: OS Explorer 158 Newbury and Hungerford.
Starting point: St Peter's church in Brimpton. GR 557647
How to get there: Follow the A4 between Woolhampton and Thatcham, turn off at the junction by the Coach and Horses and head south to Brimpton. At the T-junction in the village centre go straight over to the limited parking area by the church. If there is a church service in progress, please find an alternative parking space.
Refreshments: The Three Horseshoes lies just a couple of minutes from the walk's start and finish point on the main street of the village. The pub offers a good range of meals and snacks. Telephone: 0118 971 2183.

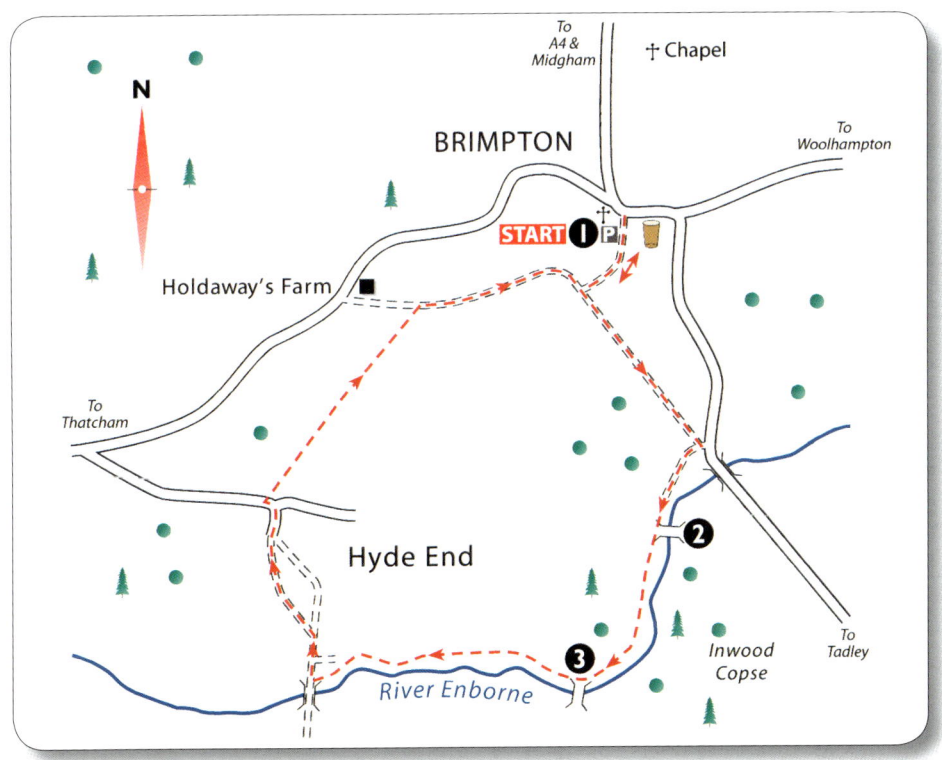

1. With your back to the main door of the village church, opposite **Elmet Cottage**, turn right and follow the footpath skirting the churchyard. Along this stretch you get close-up views of 19th-century **St Peter's church**. On reaching the corner of a field, turn left and follow its perimeter. The valley of the **Enborne** can be picked out ahead. Follow the track down through the fields to reach the road. As you approach it, turn right to follow another track, passing through a galvanised gate. Continue on the track as it skirts a field, keeping woodland over to the right.

2. On reaching a bridge on the left, avoid it and keep ahead for about 50 yards to a waymark. Swing left at this point, crossing a small bridge. Avoid going diagonally across the meadow. Instead, follow the path round its left perimeter, with the waters of the **river Enborne** beside you. Make for a gap on the left taking you into the next meadow and keep ahead with the river alongside you. After about 60 yards, veer away from the water to cross the meadow, rejoining the meandering Enborne by a gate on the far side. Cross the next meadow to a bridge set against a curtain of trees. Don't cross the bridge. Instead, turn right as you approach it, keeping the river on your left.

3. Head towards some houses, passing through trees to reach a cottage and a pond. Continue skirting the meadows to reach the next footbridge. Again don't cross it but instead walk ahead along the obvious bridle track. Pass imposing **Hyde End House** and when you reach **Oak Cottage** on the right, turn right just beyond it to follow a path between two properties, avoiding a path running off sharp right. In wintertime you can easily spot the spire of **Brimpton church** ahead between the trees. Cut between paddocks, passing through several gates, and soon the path runs beside telegraph poles, hedging and fencing. Continue across open farmland and when you reach a path junction, keep right towards the church. Follow the path back to the parking area.

■ *Brimpton's war memorial.* ■

4 **Bucklebury**
A Bit of a Puff

■ *Bucklebury's delightful village church.* ■

The Pang valley is one of the county's undiscovered treasures and is a perfect landscape for exploring on foot. Once visited, this lovely tract of Berkshire countryside will entice you back again and again, and each time you return, expect to find a new stream to roam beside or a secret wood to savour. There is a vast and complex network of paths in the valley, many of them leading to, or running beside, its enchanting river, famous throughout the country as a winter-bourne tributary of the Thames. The two rivers meet at nearby Pangbourne.

A bit of puff is required as you meander up the valley slopes towards Sadgrove Farm, though it's never a steep climb. The descent to Bucklebury Farm Park, a popular family visitor attraction famous for its deer and wild boar grazing in the fields, is when you'll begin to reap the reward. Not only does the path leave the hill climbing behind at this stage, but it offers attractive views of the Pang valley.

GRADE: 1
ESTIMATED CALORIE BURN: 500

Distance: 3 miles
Stiles: 2
Time: 2 hours
Map: OS Explorer 158 Newbury and Hungerford.
Starting point: The Victory Room car park in Bucklebury. GR 552707
How to get there: From the A4 at Thatcham head north along Hartshill Road for Bucklebury. Go through the village of Upper Bucklebury and turn left midway across Bucklebury Common for Bucklebury village. Descend to a junction, keep left to the church and turn right just beyond it. The Victory Room car park is on the left after a few yards.
Refreshments: There are no refreshment points on the route of the walk but the Boot at Stanford Dingley is only a mile or so away to the east and is an ideal watering hole. The inn offers a good range of beers and traditional pub food. Telephone: 0118 974 5213.

1 From the car park by the **Victory Room** turn right at the road, then swing right again at the signpost for **Marlston** and **Hermitage**. After Bucklebury's last house on the left, cross the stile and follow the field boundary. Soon the path cuts between trees and pastures, gradually becoming more enclosed as it heads uphill out of the **Pang valley**. Pass through a gate and continue through woodland to a pass another gate where there is a path which is not a public right of way. Just beyond it is a gate and waymark on the right.

Take this path and at the edge of the wood cross a path and go diagonally left in the field. Keep to the left of a solitary oak tree and veer left when you reach the hedge boundary just beyond it. Turn right after several paces to cross a footbridge and then turn left towards the outbuildings of **Sadgrove Farm**, seen in the distance. Keep along the field edge, pass a waymark and at the next footpath sign, head diagonally across the field corner, passing to the left of the farm buildings. Keep alongside a fence enclosing a grassy area and at the farm entrance turn left to follow a track.

2 Pass a cottage on the left and continue on the byway, avoiding a footpath running off to the left. Follow the track up between holly trees and bushes to reach a fork. Keep left here and continue to a junction with a track. With a byway opposite, turn left and walk down to a cottage – **Vanners**. As the track enters woodland, branch right to a gate and then just beyond it pass through a kissing gate on the right.

3 Head down the field towards **Bucklebury Farm Park**. Negotiate several gates before crossing a stile to join the main access drive. Pass through a

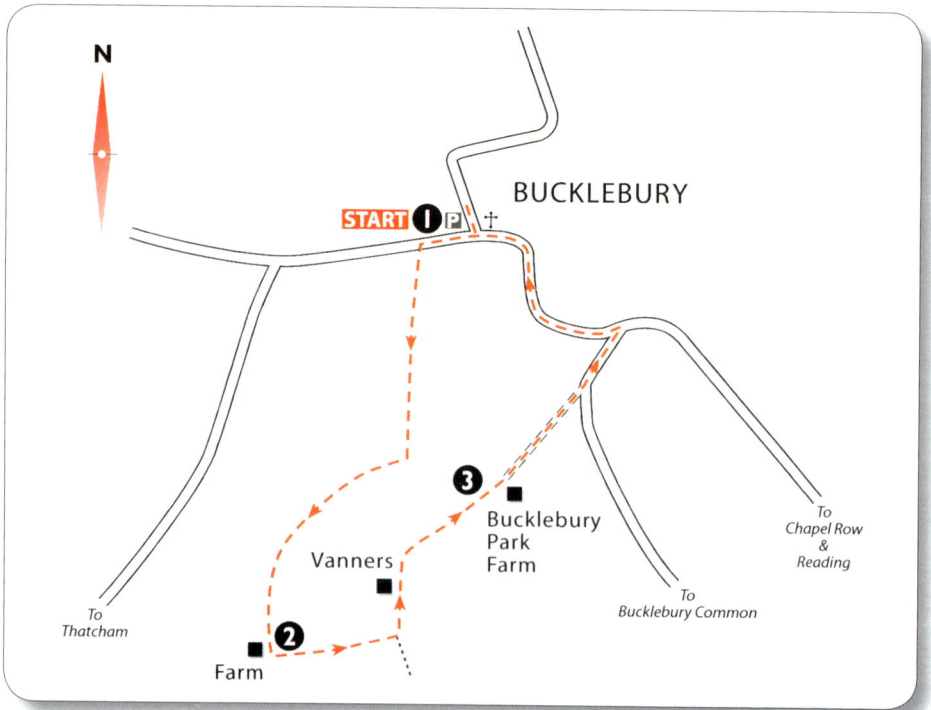

■ *Cottages in Bucklebury.* ■

kissing gate beside it, cross the drive at this point to a second kissing gate and make for the far left corner of the field. On reaching the road, turn left, then left again at the next junction. Follow the road through **Bucklebury** village, back to the car park.

25

■ *The pub at the start of the walk.* ■

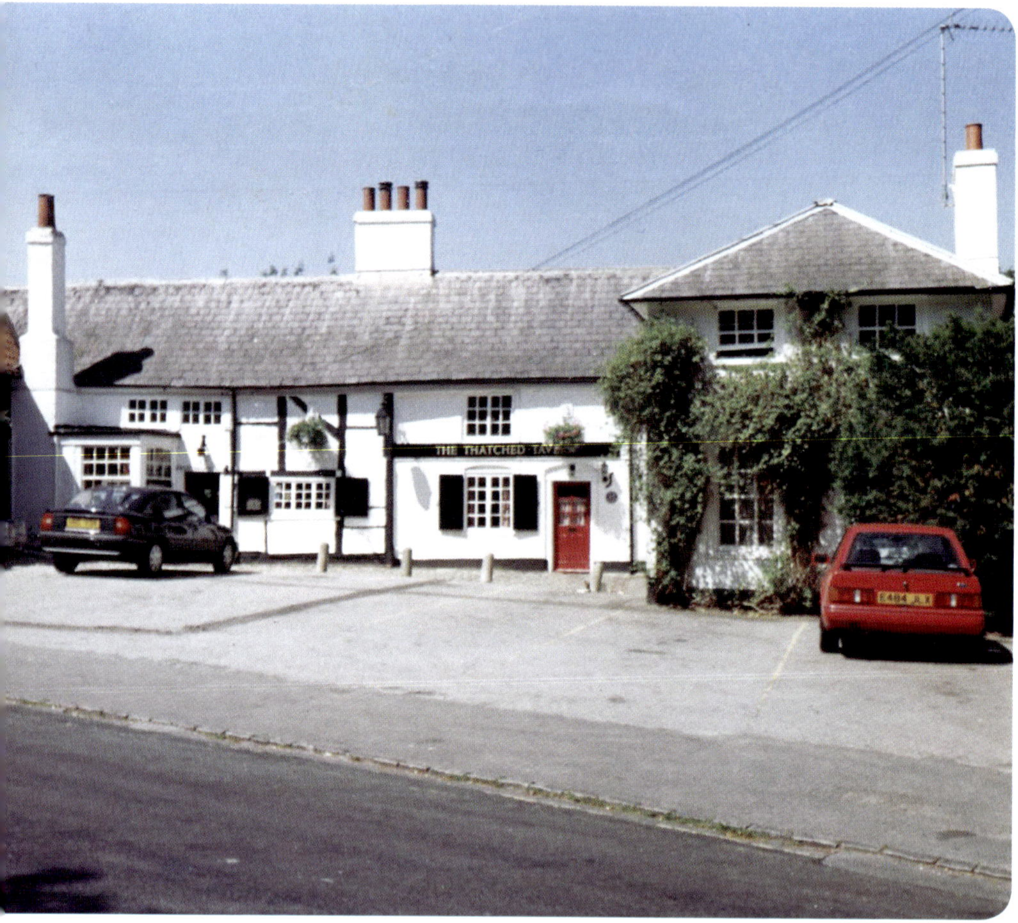

Even beginners should find themselves going at a bit of a lick on this gentle circuit – one that should give you a healthy glow without leaving you drained. Much of east Berkshire is densely populated but here and there are some surprising and truly delightful green spaces. Just a few minutes from the centre of Ascot and the county's busy motorways, the route stays mainly within the boundaries of Silwood Park, a campus of Imperial College in London.

However, there are other landmarks and attractions to capture your interest. For example St Michael and All Angels church at Sunninghill. At the main door is a plaque which reads: 'The Norman arch of the original 12th-century church was restored to this position in the year 1926.' If you're feeling energetic and want to extend the walk, there is the chance to follow a path out onto Ascot Heath. If this stretch of the walk seems familiar, that is because members of the Royal Family gather here to process by carriage to Royal Ascot every June.

GRADE: 1
ESTIMATED CALORIE BURN: 380

Distance: 2¼ miles
Stiles: None
Time: 1½ hours
Map: OS Explorer 160 Windsor, Weybridge and Bracknell.
Starting point: The Thatched Tavern car park on Cheapside Road. GR 944695
How to get there: From Bracknell follow the A329 towards Windsor Great Park. At Sunninghill turn left onto the B383 road, then left again into Cheapside Road. There is room to park in the vicinity of the Thatched Tavern.
Refreshments: The Thatched Tavern, at the start and finish of this walk, dates back to the late 15th century and includes a quaint old bar, low ceilings and a stone flagged floor. Telephone: 01344 620874.

1 From the parking area near the **Thatched Tavern pub** and with your back to the inn, turn left and walk down the road to the junction. Turn right and head for a path on the right just beyond the entrance to **Herons Brook**. Follow the path ahead through the trees; either side of it are the extensive grounds of **Silwood Park**. Continue through woodland, catching glimpses of the park between the trees. Eventually the path emerges from the woodland and heads for **Sunninghill church**. Make for the main entrance, where there is vehicular access, and take the path opposite, following it between bushes, trees and banks of vegetation.

2 Cross a stream and further on you cut between trees and paddocks. The path heads for the road and at this point turn right. Away to the left is a

■ *St Michael and All Angels 12th-century church at Sunninghill.* ■

path running to **Ascot Heath**. Back on the main walk, continue along the road and on the immediate left is an imposing gateway heralding the start of a broad grassy ride running to the famous racecourse. Continue on the road, keep ahead at the junction with **New Mile Road** and pass **Watersplash Lane**. Take the next footpath on the right and once again the walk passes through the grounds of **Silwood Park**. Drop down through the trees and on reaching a junction, turn left to the road. Turn left, then left again at the next junction and retrace your steps back to the parking area by the **Thatched Tavern**.

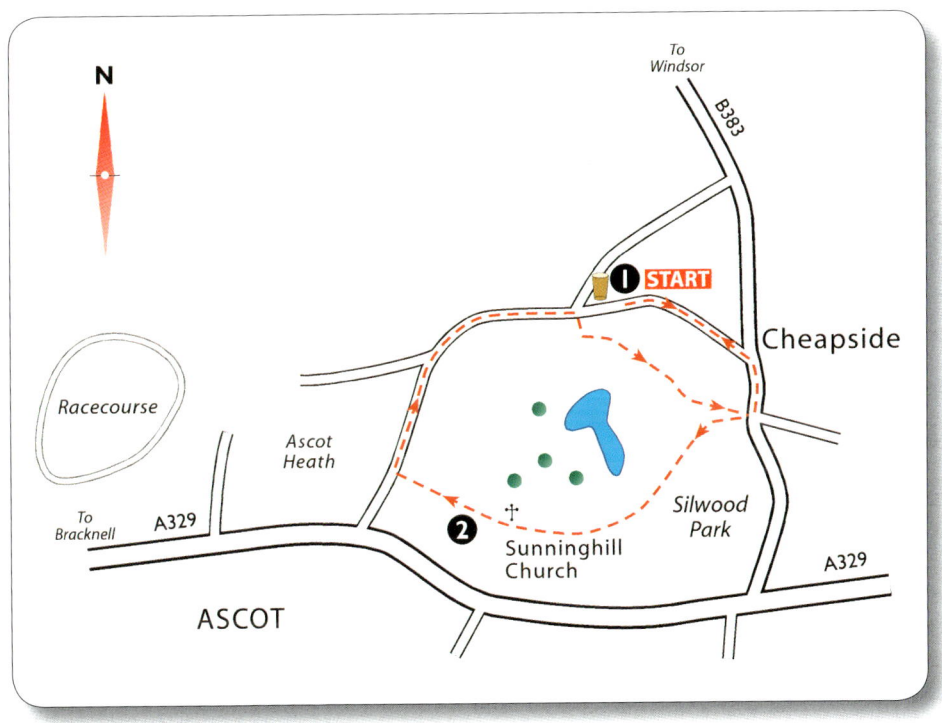

6 Cookham

Inspiration for an Artist

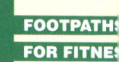

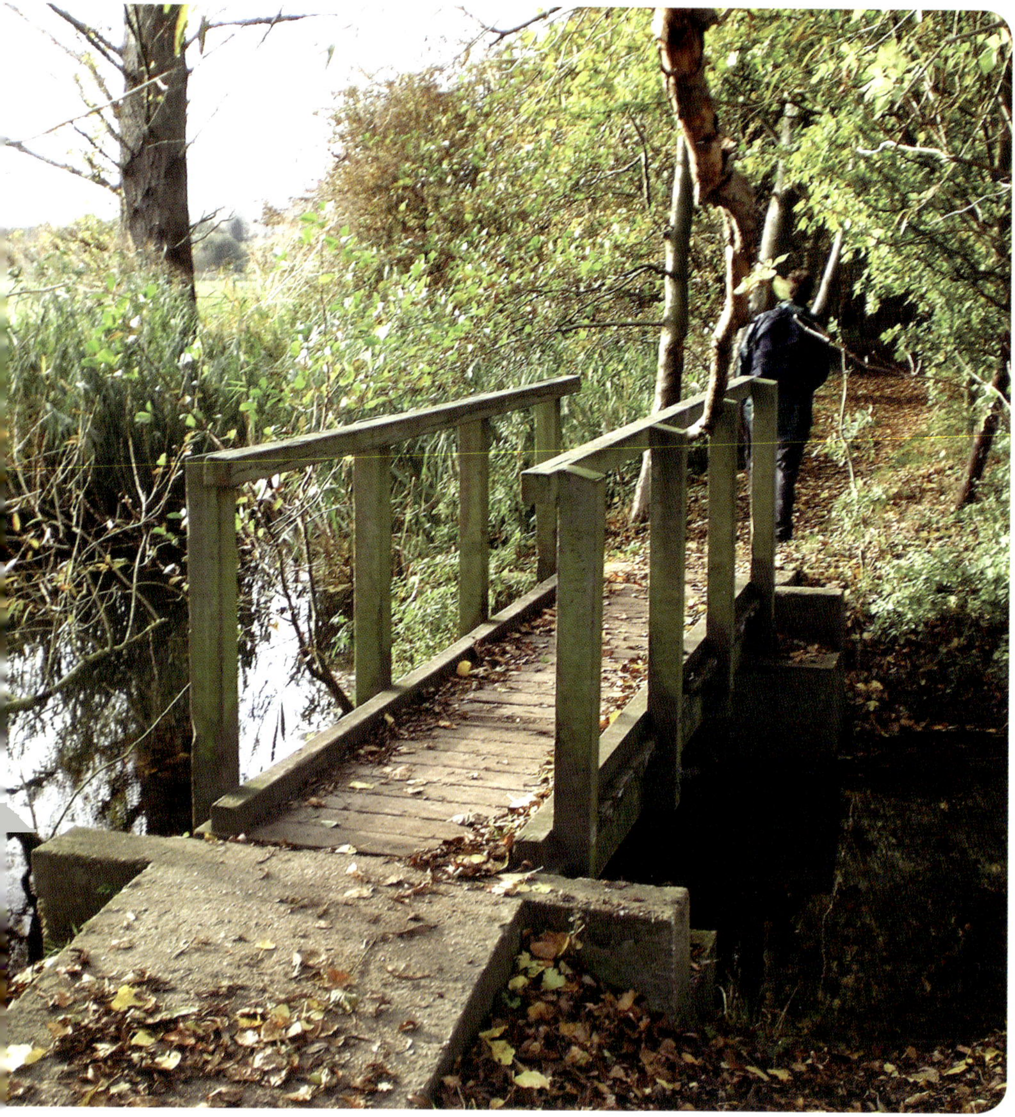

Crossing Strand Water.

With its **Stanley Spencer gallery**, handsome period houses and picturesque Thames setting, Cookham is an obvious destination for tourists. However, there is more to the village than the casual visitor might think. Cookham is the starting point for several well-publicised tourist walking trails and lesser-known circular walks. Have a look at the village, visit the gallery and then take a short, easy stroll to the south, exploring acres of quiet farmland bisected by lazy, meandering streams.

GRADE: 1
ESTIMATED CALORIE BURN: 350

Distance: 2 miles
Stiles: 2
Time: 1 – 1½ hours
Map: OS Explorer 172 Chiltern Hills East.
Starting point: The car park on Cookham Moor. GR 894853
How to get there: Cookham lies about 3½ miles north of Maidenhead on the A4094. Turn into the High Street (B4447) and the entrance to the car park on Cookham Moor is on the right on the far side of the village.
Refreshments: The Bel and the Dragon is a cosy and inviting village pub, with wooden tables and an open fire. Telephone: 01628 521263.

1 From the car park on **Cookham Moor** cross the road to a grassy embankment and turn left. Pass a pub, the **Crown**, and turn right into **School Lane**. Turn immediately right and then left at the sign for **Green Way East**. Pass alongside a brick wall and buildings before skirting a field through a tunnel of trees. Continue on the path beside a wrought-iron railing. Swing right at one point and keep ahead across farmland, with railing on the right. Continue to the next clump of trees, cross a track and keep to the right of a large field with houses visible on the far side. To the right of the path is **Strand Water**. Continue along the edge of fields until you reach a waymark in the field corner. Turn right here, across the footbridge, and skirt a reed-choked stream to the next footbridge.

2 Don't cross the concrete bridge; instead turn right in front of it over a stile and pass beside paddocks. Avoid a path on the left along here and continue until you draw level with houses on the left. Look for a stile in the fence ahead, slightly to the right of the field corner. Cross a track lined by trees, go through a gate and continue on the enclosed path, following the **Green Way West**. Continue on the trail between fields. Along this

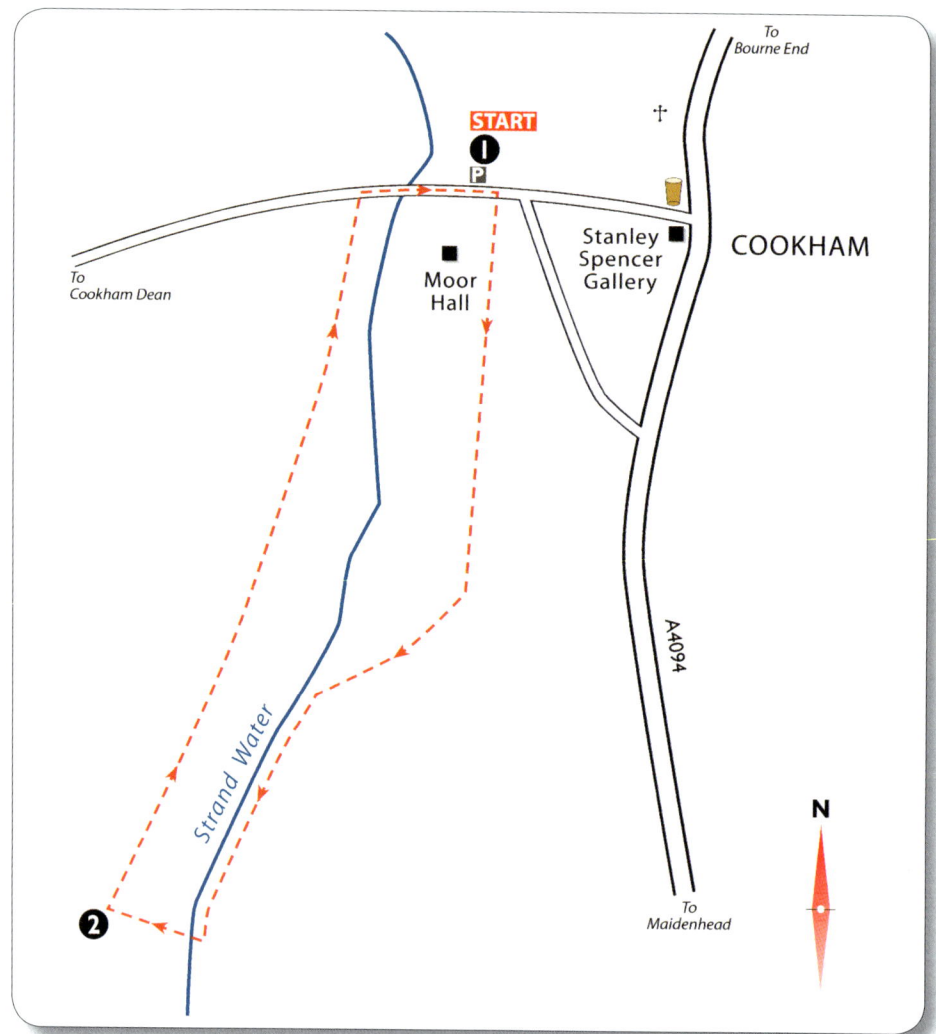

stretch are glimpses of **Cliveden**, the famous National Trust house, rising between the trees on the horizon. Make for a galvanised gate, follow the path ahead through a tunnel of trees and go through several gates to pass beside a laurel hedge. Pass some loose boxes and follow a stony drive to a gate leading out to the road. Turn right and return to the car park on **Cookham Moor**.

■ *On the way back to Cookham.* ■

7 Wokingham
On the Heritage Trail

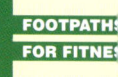

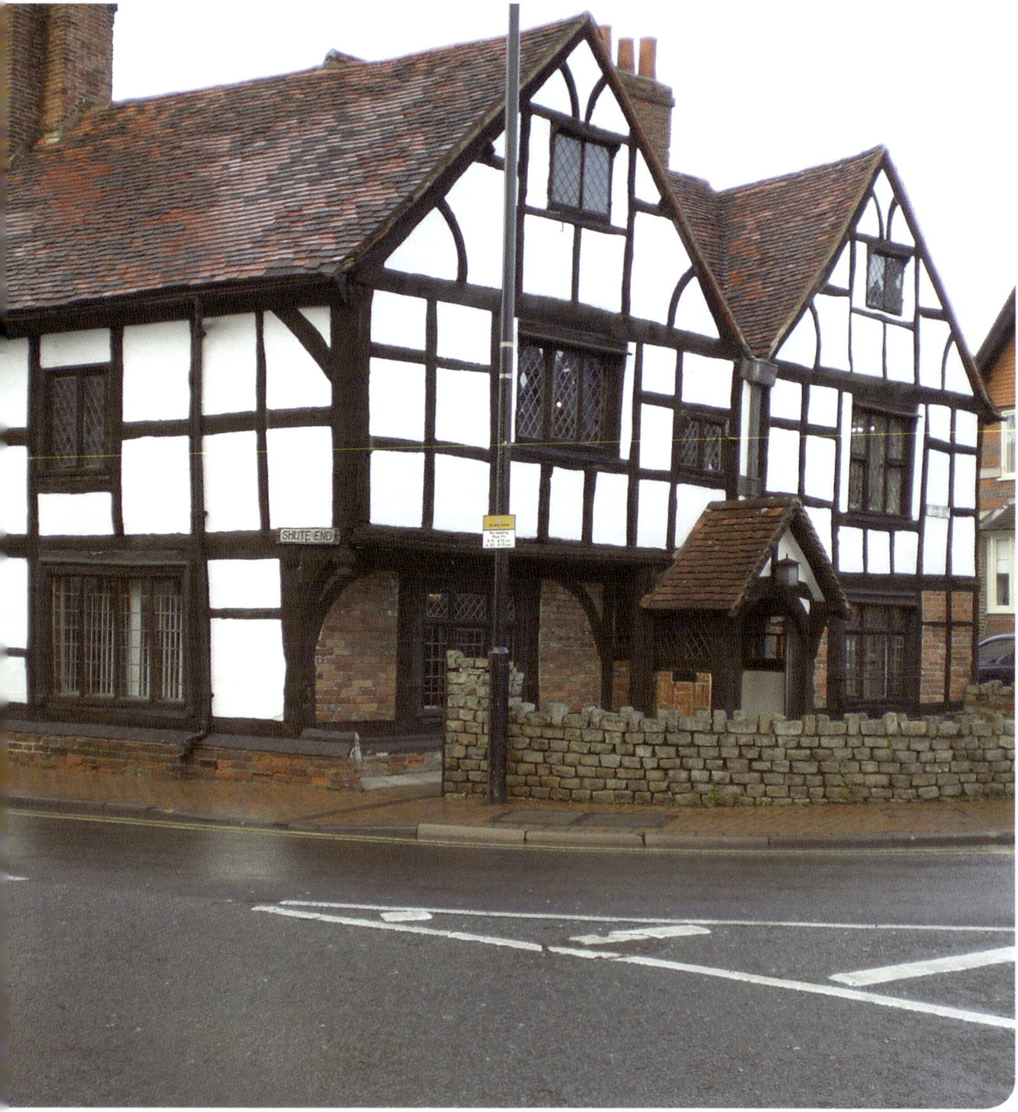

The ancient Tudor House.

Rambling in the countryside is rewarding and tranquil. Town walking is a completely different experience. Hardly a minute goes by when there isn't something to crave your attention – a period building perhaps, a leafy square or an imposing statue to a local benefactor. Whatever it offers, a town heritage trail is a stimulating and fascinating experience. With its hidden corners and picturesque old buildings, the east Berkshire town of Wokingham is the perfect place to explore on foot. Founded in the 13th century by the Norman-French bishop Roger le Poore, the town was granted a charter by Queen Elizabeth I in 1583. One of Wokingham's most attractive buildings, the Tudor House, dates back to the mid 16th century. The front was partly altered in the early 20th century by incorporating timbers from a dismantled mansion nearby.

GRADE: 1
ESTIMATED CALORIE BURN: 340

Distance: 2 miles
Stiles: None
Time: 1 – 1½ hours
Maps: OS Explorer 159 Reading, Wokingham and Pangbourne. Ideally, use a good street map of Wokingham which can be obtained from the tourist information centre in the Town Hall.
Starting point: The Town Hall in Wokingham's market place. GR 813685
How to get there: From junction 10 of the M4 east of Reading follow the signs for the town centre. There are several public car parks within easy reach of the Market Place. Wokingham has its own railway station on the Reading to Waterloo line. The station is in Station Road, at the end of Broad Street.
Refreshments: Piazza Café in the Town Hall is a handy refreshment stop at the start and finish of the walk. Telephone: 0118 979 4368. The 16th-century Metropolitan in Rose Street is a traditional town pub midway round the walk. Telephone: 0118 979 1825.

1 From the 19th-century triangular town hall in the **Market Place** walk along **Broad Street**, passing **Rose Street** on the right. On the left is the Nationwide Building Society which was once the setting for Wokingham's first cinema. It opened in 1912 as the Electric Theatre and later became the Savoy before closing in the 1950s. Head for **Central Walk**, the site of the town's old brewery which closed at the beginning of the First World War.

Pass handsome Oxford House and cross over into **Milton Road**. On the corner is the 16th-century Tudor House and to the right is the police station, built in 1904. With its distinctive pagoda-like towers and ornate chimneys, the building is a well-known landmark in Wokingham. Follow **Milton Road** alongside the Baptist church and on reaching **Glebelands Road**, turn right to follow a leafy, residential section of the walk.

2 Turn right at the main T-junction into **Rectory Road** and swing sharp left to join a path just before the Waitrose supermarket car park. Turn left at the next road, then almost immediately right at the footpath sign (avoiding the signposted path running straight on) and follow the path through **Rose Gardens** to **Rose Court** – a small close of houses built in the middle of the 19th century. Turn left at **Rose Street**, one of Wokingham's hidden treasures and possibly the finest example of an enclosed street in Berkshire. James 'Sooty' Seaward lived here and was the inspiration for Tom the chimney sweep in Charles Kingsley's classic children's story *The Water Babies*. Walk down to **All Saints' church**, originally a small Saxon chapel and enlarged in the 12th century.

3 Turn right and right again at the **Ship Inn**. Pass **Easthampstead Road** and turn left into **South Place**. Swing right by the fire station to follow **Denton**

■ *Rose Street, Wokingham.* ■

Road. Ahead is a car park. Walk through it to the far end and turn right at **Langborough Road** to the **Duke's Head**, originally several cottages. Turn right at the roundabout and pass the old Memorial Orthopaedic Clinic on the left, given to the town in memory of the men who fell in battle. Follow **Denmark Street** and return to the triangular **Market Place**, passing **Erftstadt Court**, once the site of a brewery and the old Territorial Army drill hall.

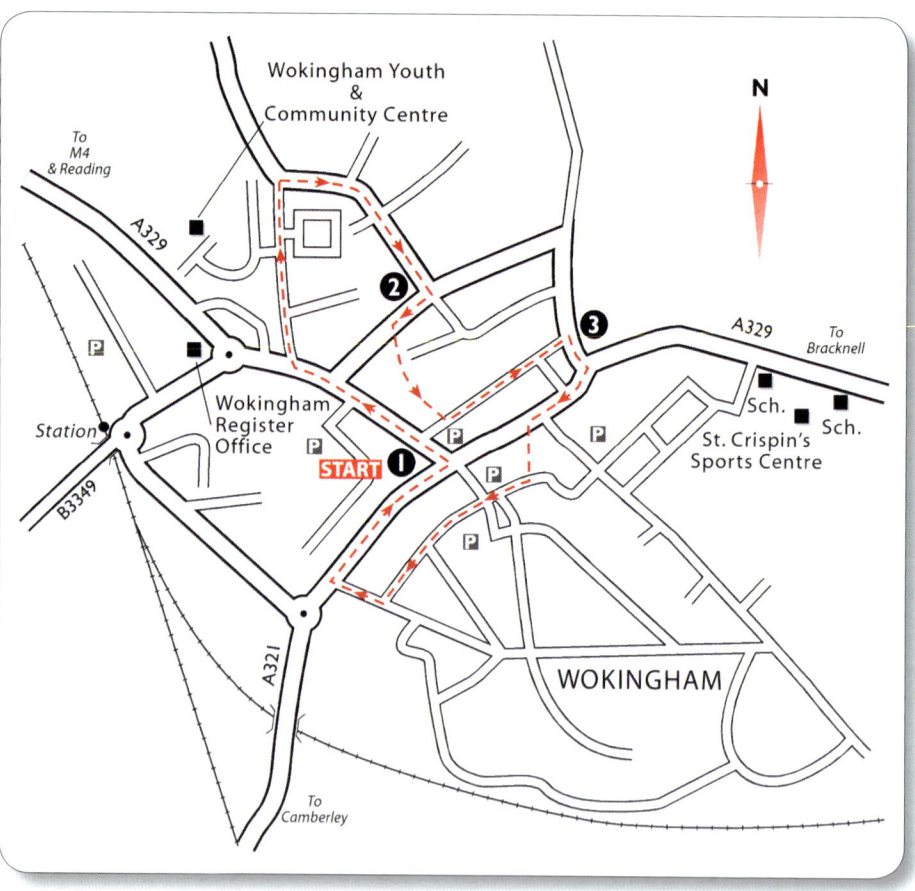

8 *East Ilsley*
On Ancient Paths

■ *On the Berkshire downs.* ■

A **short section of the Ridgeway** is one of the key features on this spectacular downland walk. The wild, solitary country to the north of Newbury, a natural walker's playground, is bisected by Britain's oldest road, now one of the country's most popular national trails. Here, an intricate maze of paths and tracks takes you to the heart of the Berkshire downs, and a careful study of the Ordnance Survey map provides ideas for walks of all shapes and sizes. If you are feeling particularly adventurous and energetic, you could even follow the Ridgeway from East Ilsley all the way to Avebury in Wiltshire or across the Thames and through the Chilterns to its most northerly point in Buckinghamshire.

The route I have chosen, however, is relatively short and, on the whole, undemanding. But this is adventure country and even a more modest walk here evokes a sense of real drama, demonstrating quite graphically the harshness of this terrain. In the depths of winter, on a bitterly cold and frosty day, you'll find few other souls on the walk. There are also few opportunities to shelter from the wind and rain so take plenty of protective clothing.

GRADE: 2
ESTIMATED CALORIE BURN: 580

Distance: 3½ miles
Stiles: None
Time: 1½ – 2 hours
Map: OS Explorer 170 Abingdon, Wantage and Vale of White Horse.
Starting point: the village pond in East Ilsley. GR 493812
How to get there: From Oxford or Newbury, take the A34 and East Ilsley is signposted north of the M4. Follow the road into the village and park in the vicinity of the pond.
Refreshments: The Crown and Horns at East Ilsley serves a range of wholesome and appetising meals and snacks – just the place after a winter walk on the downs. Telephone: 01635 281205.

---

1 Keep the village pond on your left, turn left into **Haydon Lane** and pass the **Old Rectory**. On a fine autumn day, the trees along this stretch are glorious. When the tarmac lane swings right, keep ahead on a byway, passing footpaths on the left and right. The track leaves the village of **East Ilsley** behind. Ahead and to the right are striking views over fields and open downland. At a junction with a byway, turn left and follow the track between hedges to reach the road. Cross over and continue on the next

■ The Crown and Horns at East Ilsley. ■

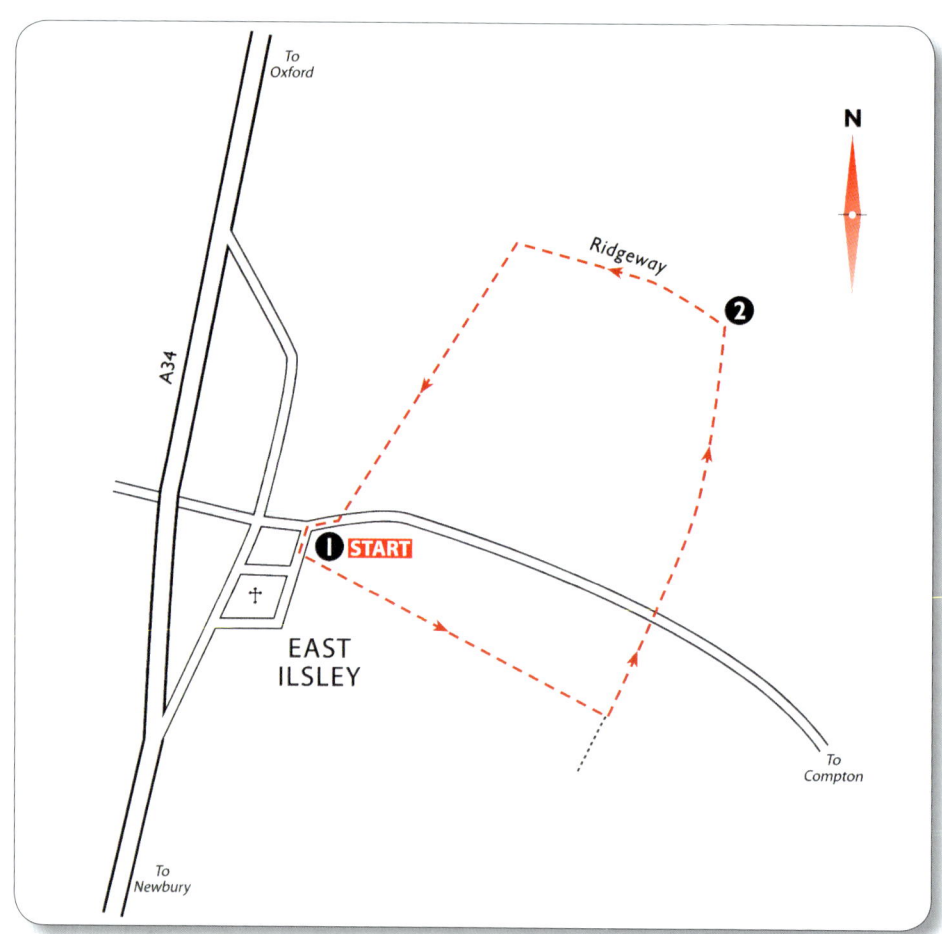

section of byway, with the buildings of **East Ilsley** glimpsed over on the left. Follow the track up the gentle slope towards a windbreak of trees, pass over a track and then between the trees to reach the next intersection. Cross over the byway and remain on the grassy track to reach the **Ridgeway**.

2 Keep left, following the concrete track with the towers of Didcot power station visible over to the right. When the track swings left to some gates, continue ahead on the **Ridgeway**. Head for a bridleway on the left, take it then head south towards **East Ilsley**. The track cuts between swathes of sweeping downland. The village houses loom into view as you follow the bridleway. Turn right at the road and return to the pond.

9 Kintbury

A Canalside Stride

FOOTPATHS FOR FITNESS

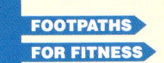

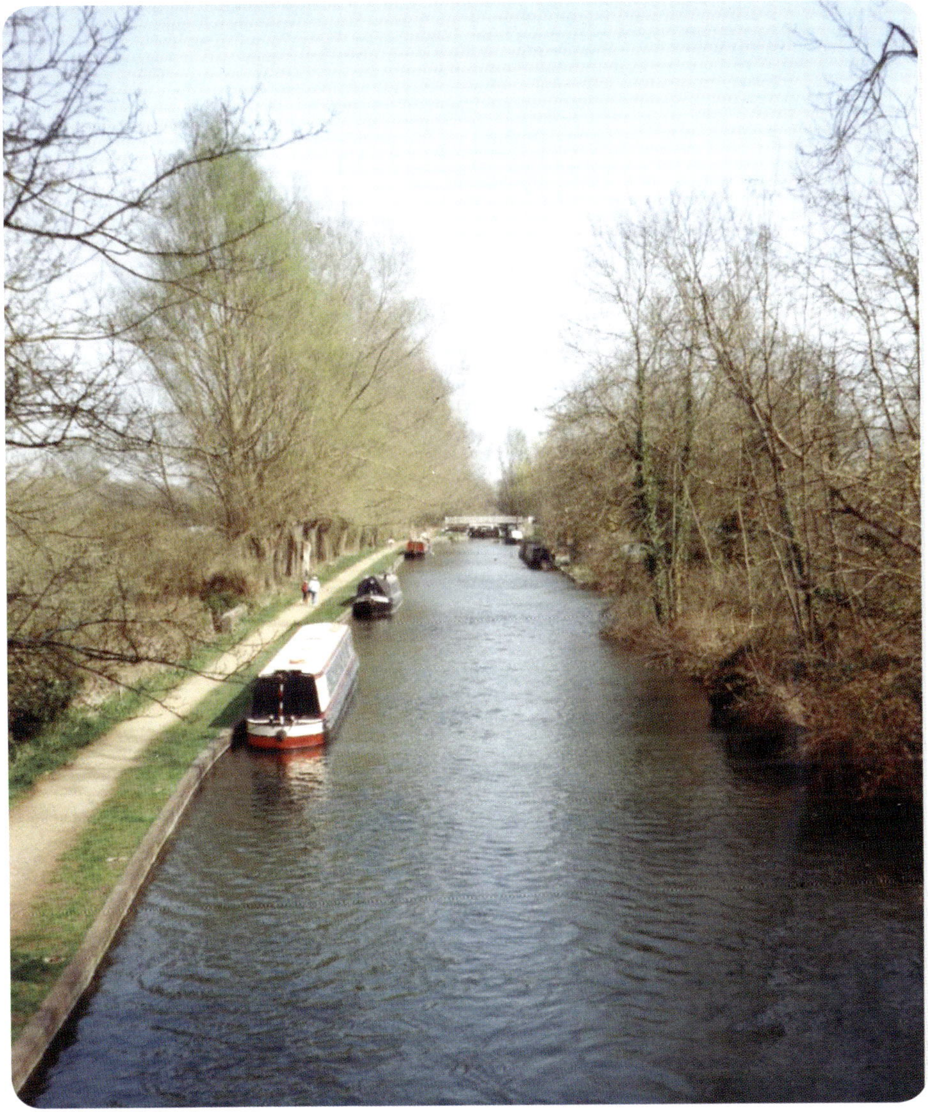

The Kennet and Avon Canal.

The story of a great inland waterway is told as you stroll its banks west towards the town of Hungerford. The Kennet and Avon Canal was opened in 1810 at a cost of £1 million. It took 16 years to complete and was built to link the Thames at Reading with the Bristol docks. After a long period in the doldrums – the railway era effectively killed it off – the canal was gradually restored and eventually reopened in the summer of 1990. Today, it is a thriving, vibrant waterway attracting boaters, walkers, cyclists and fishermen. To stroll beside the Kennet and Avon is to witness the development and renaissance of an historic inland waterway. Plenty of ramblers will share your easy waterside route on a fine summer's day but it is a different story when you leave the canal to explore the slopes of the Kennet valley. The scenery here, a fine mix of secluded woodland and lush pasture, entices the walker. There are several undemanding ascents and some rough terrain on the valley slopes but the going is never especially hard.

GRADE: 2
ESTIMATED CALORIE BURN: 860

Distance: 5 miles
Stiles: 12
Time: 2 hours
Map: OS Explorer 158 Newbury and Hungerford.
Starting point: The car park near Kintbury station. GR 385672
How to get there: Follow the A4 between Newbury and Hungerford and take the turning for Kintbury. Cross the railway and then turn immediately right into the public car park. There is a station next to the car park, with regular train services between Great Bedwyn, Newbury and Reading.
Refreshments: The Dundas Arms, just across the water from the village car park, is named after Charles Dundas, the first chairman of the Kennet and Avon Canal company. As well as the bar, there is a most attractive terrace overlooking the water. In summer this can get very busy, but if you can secure a table here it is well worth it in order to watch all the colourful activity on the canal. Telephone: 01488 658263.

1 From the car park join the towpath and turn right, keeping the canal on your left-hand side. Pass beneath a brick bridge, cross a concrete bridge over a side channel and continue on the towpath. Keep ahead to the next bridge where there is a seat. Leave the towpath here, cross the bridge and

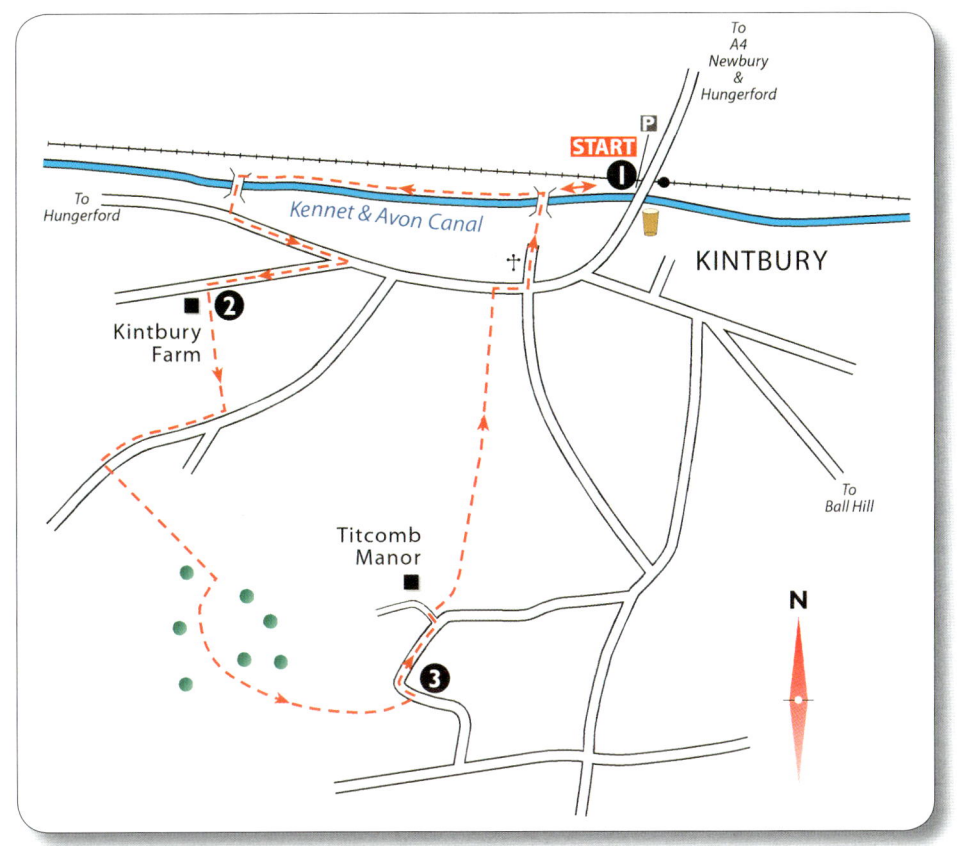

follow the track to the road. Turn left here and when the road bends left, turn sharp right in the direction of Inkpen and Templeton. Pass **Templeton House** to a footpath on the left by **Kintbury Farm**.

2 Take the path, skirting a field to keep beside trees and a hedgerow. Make for a gate in the field corner, keep ahead in the next pasture and when the track curves right, go straight on, keeping to the right of several telegraph poles. On reaching a tarmac lane, turn right and after about 60 yards you come to a footpath crossing. Turn right into the field and then veer diagonally left towards **St Cassian's College**. Head for a line of young trees, cross a stile here and walk ahead to a footpath sign. Turn sharp left and keep St Cassian's on the right. On reaching brick pillars at the entrance, cross the drive to the remains of a wrought-iron kissing-gate. Veer right at the fork after a few yards and pass through a plantation to the next stile. Follow a broad grassy ride between trees, cross a stile into a field and head to the next stile, avoiding a path running off to the left. Continue in the field towards trees, cross the next stile and keep the woodland close by on the right. Descend to a pair of stiles in the trees by the right boundary, pass through a gap into the field on the right and head diagonally up the slope to a stile. Join a tarmac drive and walk down the slope to a cattle grid.

3 Turn left at the sign for **Titcomb Manor**, avoid a footpath on the right and on reaching a gate at the entrance to the manor, turn right over a stile. Turn left after a few yards and walk alongside fencing. On reaching a galvanised gate and a footpath sign, swing right and keep the fence to your left. Cross a stile in the bottom corner of the field and continue with hedging on the right to a gate. Follow a path skirting woodland to a footbridge and stile, veer over to the left for several steps to the next stile and follow the woodland path all the way to the road at **Kintbury**. Turn right, then left into **Church Street** and walk down towards the church. Veer to the right of it, still on the road, and walk down to the entrance to the Old Rectory. Turn right at this point, cross the canal and then turn immediately right, down to the towpath. Follow it ahead for a short distance and return to the car park.

■ *The attractive Dundas Arms.* ■

■ *Pointing the way at Catmore.* ■

There is some gentle climbing on this superb downland walk which explores one of the more remote corners of rural Berkshire – perfect for blowing away the cobwebs after the excesses of Christmas.

Alternatively, a sunny day in spring is the ideal time for completing the circuit, when this wonderful walking country is bursting into life again after the dormant months of winter. Whatever time of the year, you might like to visit the isolated settlement of Catmore where you can follow a path through the farmyard to St Margaret's church. Though the church was made redundant in 1973, there are three services a year – an evensong at Whitsun, a harvest festival and a carol service on Christmas Eve.

GRADE: 2
ESTIMATED CALORIE BURN: 750

Distance: 4½ miles
Stiles: 4
Time: 2 hours
Map: OS Explorer 170 Abingdon, Wantage and the Vale of the White Horse.
Starting point: By the church in Farnborough. GR 435819
How to get there: Follow the B4494 road between Newbury and Wantage and turn off at the sign for Farnborough. Drive through the village and park outside the church at the point where the road bends left.
Refreshments: The Harrow at nearby West Ilsley, about two miles north-east of Catmore, occupies the perfect village location. Across the road is the village cricket ground which means in summer the pub tends to fill up with players and enthusiasts. Telephone: 01635 281260.

1 Cross the stile by the parking area on the bend in the road and veer left across the middle of the field. **The Old Rectory**, the home between 1945 and 1951 of Poet Laureate John Betjeman and his wife Penelope, is clearly visible to the north. Follow the path to the right-hand corner of the pasture and cross a stile. Head diagonally left across this field with good views of **Beacon Hill** and the Hampshire hills down to the south. Make for a stile in the hedge and in the next field keep left alongside a line of trees and bushes. On reaching a waymark after about 80 yards, keep right and follow the bridle track across open fields and downland. Head down the slope, following the path as it curves slightly right. Make for a hedge, pass through the gap and keep ahead at a grassy track on a bend. Woodland, with a number of silver birch trees, makes up the scene on the right. Continue ahead at the next bridleway intersection and climb gradually to reach the road.

■ *The Old Rectory seen from the route.* ■

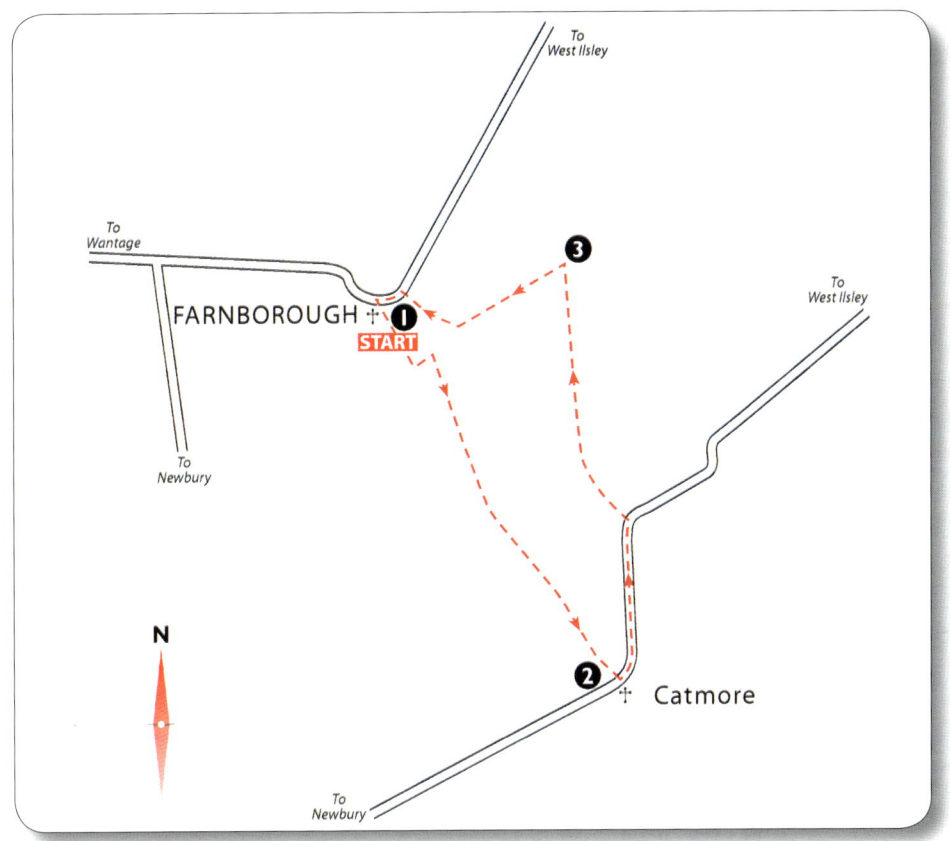

2 Turn right for **Catmore** and soon you come to a sign for **St Margaret's church**. Follow the signs to visit the church and then return to the road by the same route. Turn right, pass the track followed on the outward leg of the walk and continue up the road. Pass a pond and follow the road as it bends left. At the next right-hand bend, keep left to join a track, following what is known as the **Three Downs Link**. Keep to the broad path as it cuts through trees. Pass over a junction and continue ahead.

3 Beyond the wood, where the path is flanked by hedges, take a left-hand path and cross a stile. Cross farmland with glimpses to the right of a house aptly named **Lands End**. Go straight on when you reach the corner of a field and keep ahead towards **Farnborough**. With the field perimeter on your right, pass to the left of a water tower before reaching the road. Keep left and return to the car parking area by the village church.

11 Bagnor
Treading the Boards

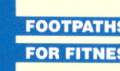

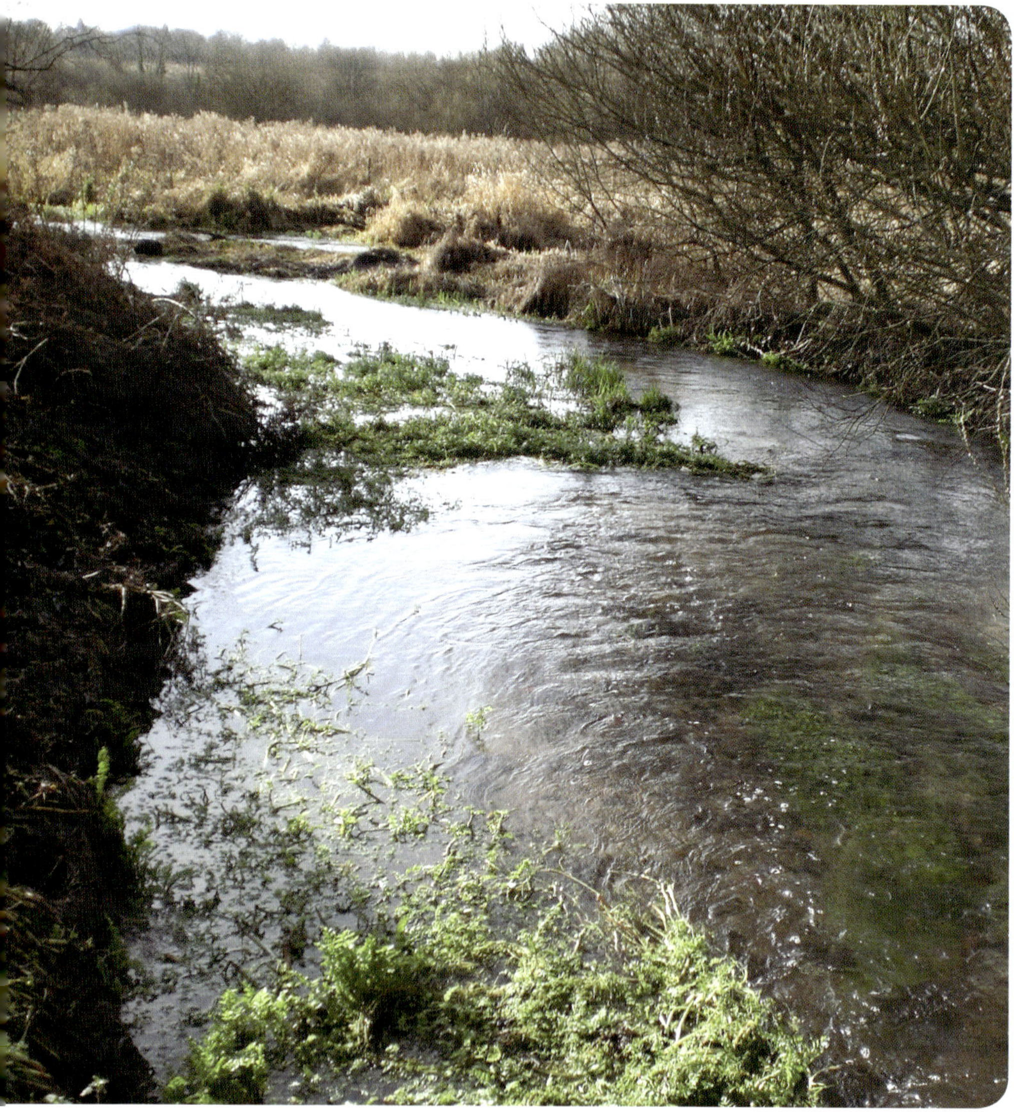

■ *The River Lambourn.* ■

Whether you are a novice walker or a dedicated hiker, a good country pub is an essential ingredient on a country ramble. This fairly undemanding route through the Lambourn valley offers two excellent hostelries – one at the start, the other midway round. In addition to imbibing, there is the chance to enjoy entertainment of a very different kind at the walk's start and finishing point. Not many circular walks in Britain include a theatre – especially one at the heart of the country. At Bagnor you'll find the Watermill, one of the country's most prestigious and respected provincial theatres. The building is mid 19th century, though there has been a mill on this site since Domesday. During the 1840s, writing paper was produced here, then, later, corn. The mill became a theatre in the mid 1960s. From Bagnor the walk is no more than an easy stroll by the river Lambourn before it begins a gentle climb out of the Lambourn valley to the neighbouring village of Stockcross. The return leg offers impressive views across the valley and there is a final stretch by the tranquil waters of the Lambourn to round off this charming circuit – highly enjoyable at any time of the year and one that will appeal to most age groups as well as anyone who is reasonably fit.

GRADE: 2
ESTIMATED CALORIE BURN: 600

Distance: 3½ miles
Stiles: 4
Time: 1 – 2 hours
Map: OS Explorer 158 Newbury and Hungerford.
Starting point: In the centre of Bagnor near the Blackbird pub. GR 454694
How to get there: Bagnor is about 2 miles to the north-west of Newbury. Follow the B4000 Lambourn road from Newbury and then turn right, signposted to Bagnor. There are distinctive brown Watermill Theatre signs. There is usually room to park by the verge in the vicinity of the Blackbird pub.
Refreshments: The Rising Sun at Stockcross is an award-winning village pub with a good reputation for home-cooked food. The inn is owned by the locally based West Berkshire Brewery. Telephone: 01488 608131. The Blackbird at Bagnor is the place to go after a walk in winter when a log fire creates a very pleasant and cosy atmosphere. Telephone: 01635 40638.

1 From the parking area in the centre of **Bagnor** follow the road ahead through the village, crossing the **river Lambourn**. Avoid the drive on the left to the **Watermill Theatre** and take the next left turning. Follow it to a stile by a gate and a traffic mirror, cross it and proceed to the next stile, taking the path ahead between fenced paddocks. Continue ahead to a stile and then follow the path beside the **Lambourn**. Here it divides into several courses to create a classic picture of rural England. Keep left at **Crossways Cottage** and follow the tarmac drive to the road.

2 Cross over into **Snake Lane**, signposted to **Stockcross**. Climb gently through the trees, following the lane between banks and hedgerows. At one point the road curves left. Swing right here to join a sunken byway which can be very muddy, keep climbing and veer right at the road. Follow it round two left bends, pass a school and then turn right into the car park of the **Rising Sun**. From the pub car park turn left and retrace your steps

■ *The prestigious* ■
Watermill Theatre.

back along the lane and beside the school. When the road bends right, go straight on along a track which is waymarked. At the point where it turns sharp left, go through a gate and follow the path ahead along the edge of the field. On reaching a byway immediately beyond a gate, turn left. There are glorious views of the Lambourn valley here. After about 70 yards the track bends right for **Woodspeen Farm**.

3 Avoid the turn and keep ahead on the signposted byway, following it between trees and gorse bushes. Follow the track round to the right and between lines of trees before descending towards **Priddles Farm**. Cross over at the road beyond it, join a footpath by a traffic mirror and head down some steps. Follow the right of way between wooden fencing, cross a stile and a bridge and take the path beside the shallow Lambourn. Cross another stile and about 40 yards beyond it turn right to follow the **Lambourn Valley Way**. Continue on the broad path through woodland, pass a stile on the left and keep ahead towards **Bagnor**. The meandering river can be seen on the right, down in the valley. On reaching the grounds of **Bagnor Manor**, turn left and follow the drive back to the start of the walk.

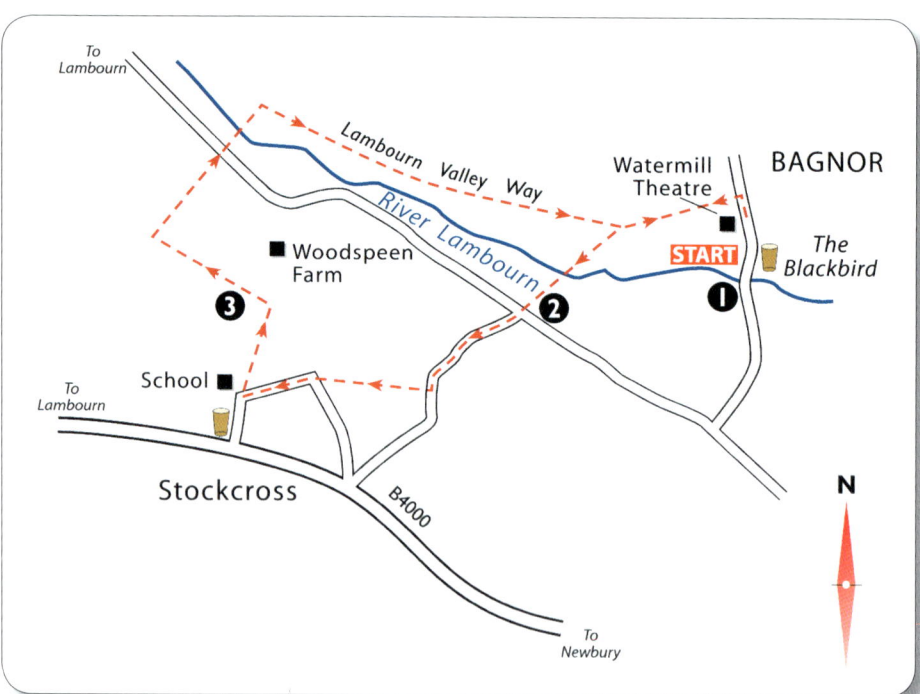

12 Pangbourne
Meadows and Woodland

FOOTPATHS FOR FITNESS

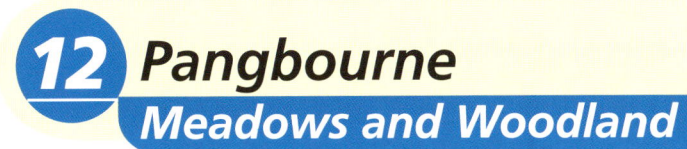

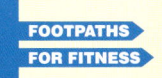

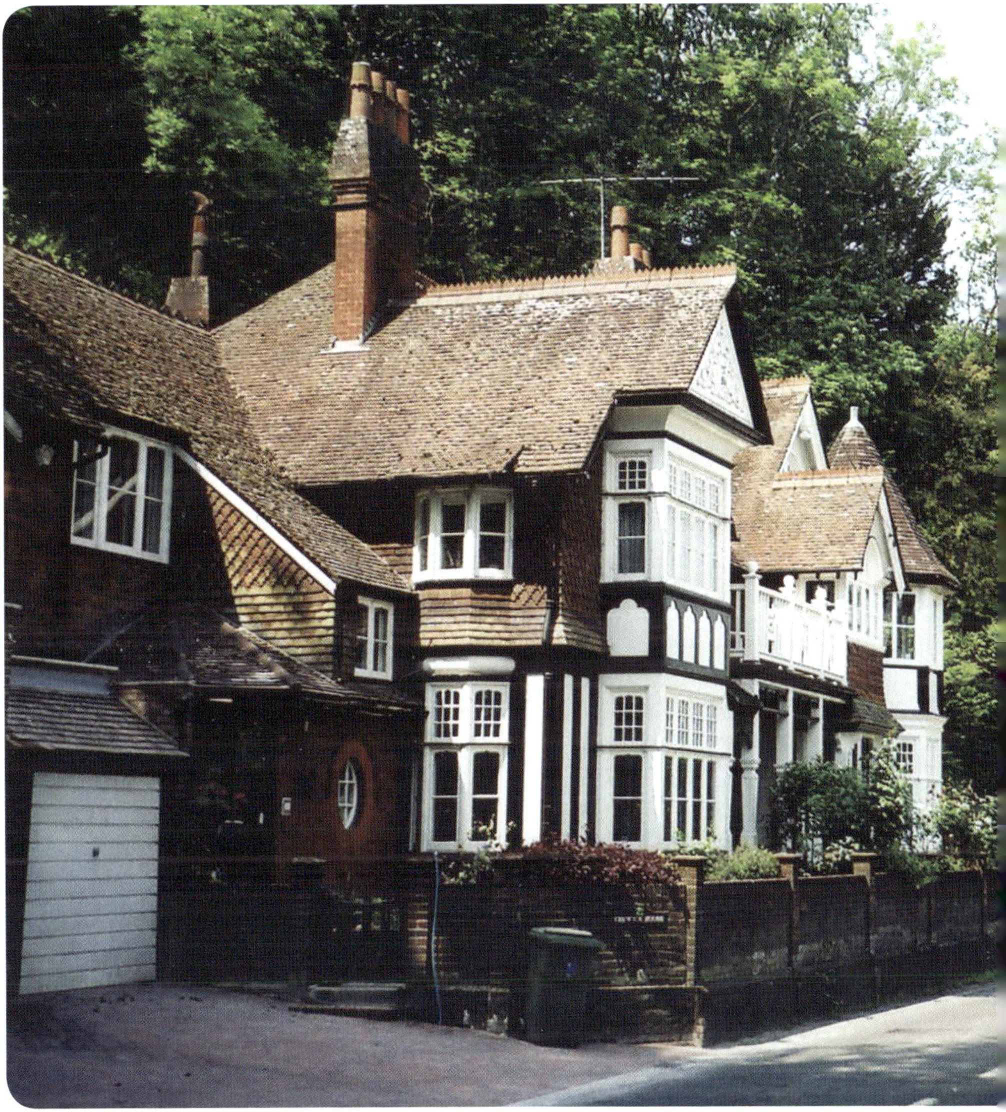

The Seven Deadly Sins.

The initial stages of this glorious valley walk are beside the meandering river Pang, close to where it meets the Thames. Meadow walking is perfect for beginners but if you want something a bit more ambitious, then leave the nursery slopes at Tidmarsh and begin a lengthy but rewarding climb out of the Pang valley to reach Pangbourne College. The going is pretty gentle, not steep, but the climb is gradual and lengthy. On the high ground the walk makes for the grounds of the college, within close proximity of the famous chapel with its Falklands Memorial Window, before reaching a road which lacks a pavement. This is a short but unavoidable section of the walk. It's not a main road but it does get busy at certain times of the day. Take care and watch the traffic. Back in the peace of the countryside again, the final leg of the circuit explores a stretch of magical woodland en route to the Thames. Join the road and follow the pavement back into Pangbourne. This is a good ramble ideally suited to those with at least some experience of walking.

■ *All aboard.* ■

GRADE: 2
ESTIMATED CALORIE BURN: 900

Distance: 5½ miles
Stiles: 2
Time: 2¾ hours
Map: OS Explorer 159 Reading, Wokingham and Pangbourne.
Starting point: The car park at Pangbourne Meadows. GR 636767
How to get there: Approach Pangbourne on either the A329 (the Reading to Wantage road) or the A340 from the south. At the mini-roundabout by WH Smith, pass under the railway and then turn right into the car park by Pangbourne Meadows. There are regular train services between Oxford and Reading.
Refreshments: The Ditty is a small café in the centre of Pangbourne and is just the place for a snack or a main meal. Telephone: 0118 984 3050. Alternatively, there are several pubs in the vicinity.

1 From the car park turn left, pass beneath the railway bridge and head for a mini-roundabout in the centre of **Pangbourne**. Make for WH Smith and turn into **The Moors** which runs alongside the shop.

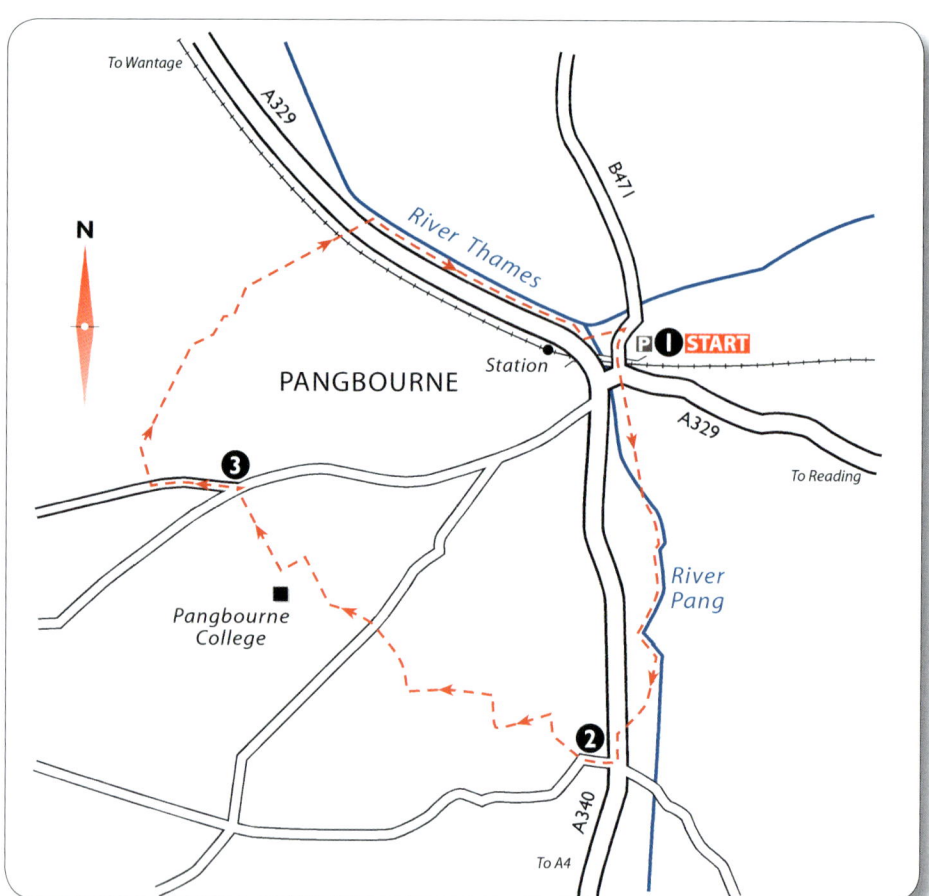

Follow the public footpath over a private road and alongside houses. On reaching a gate, take the path to the left of it and pass through a tunnel of trees. Cut between hedging and fencing to reach a gate and keep to the right of a holly tree and then beside the **Pang** as the walk crosses tranquil meadows. Continue with the river on your right, avoiding paths running off to the left, and make for a footbridge. Cross the **Pang** and then bear left. Go through a galvanised gate and continue with the river now on your left. Cross a stile by an animal shelter and continue for a few paces to another gate. At a waymark just beyond it turn left to join a drive serving houses. Continue ahead at the next stile, pass a turning on the right and at the entrance to a property called **Longbridge**, turn right. Follow the path along the field edge; soon the path becomes enclosed by trees. Keep ahead to a track, cross over and continue to the road.

2 Turn left and cross **Strachey Close** – named after the biographer and member of the Bloomsbury Group, Lytton Strachey, who lived locally. Walk through Tidmarsh to the Greyhound pub, turn right into **Tidmarsh Lane** and follow the lane to a left-hand bend. Go through the gate on the right and diagonally up the gentle slope to a gate. Pass through the gate and then follow the track ahead, keeping a line of trees on the left. Follow the track round to the left and along the field perimeter, then right in the corner to an enclosed path running off to the left. Walk between hedges and then bend right by some houses to join a track running between trees. Cross a country road and continue on a track with houses on the right. Ahead are the buildings of **Pangbourne College**. Pass through a gate and continue on tarmac to a 'Give Way' sign. Turn left along a tarmac drive and then right at the next junction. When the drive forks by a tennis court, veer left and descend to the road on a junction where the highway splits.

3 Cross to the far road and walk along a stretch of highway that can be busy at certain times of the day. There is no pavement so take extra care. Walk along to a footpath on the right and skirt the field to the corner. Pass through a gap by woodland and head diagonally across the next pasture, keeping to the left of some houses. Pass into the next field via a gateway and keep along its right-hand edge towards woodland. Make for a kissing gate in the field corner and enter the trees. Descend through the woodland, eventually reaching a railway bridge. Pass beneath it and turn right at the road. Pass the **Seven Deadly Sins**, seven very distinctive roadside houses built in the 1890s by DH Evans of the famous West End department store, and continue to the Swan. Walk towards the railway bridge and turn left just beyond it to follow a waymarked path which soon runs beside the Thames to reach the car park where the walk began.

13 Twyford

In the Steps of a Great Engineer

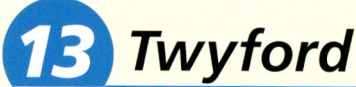

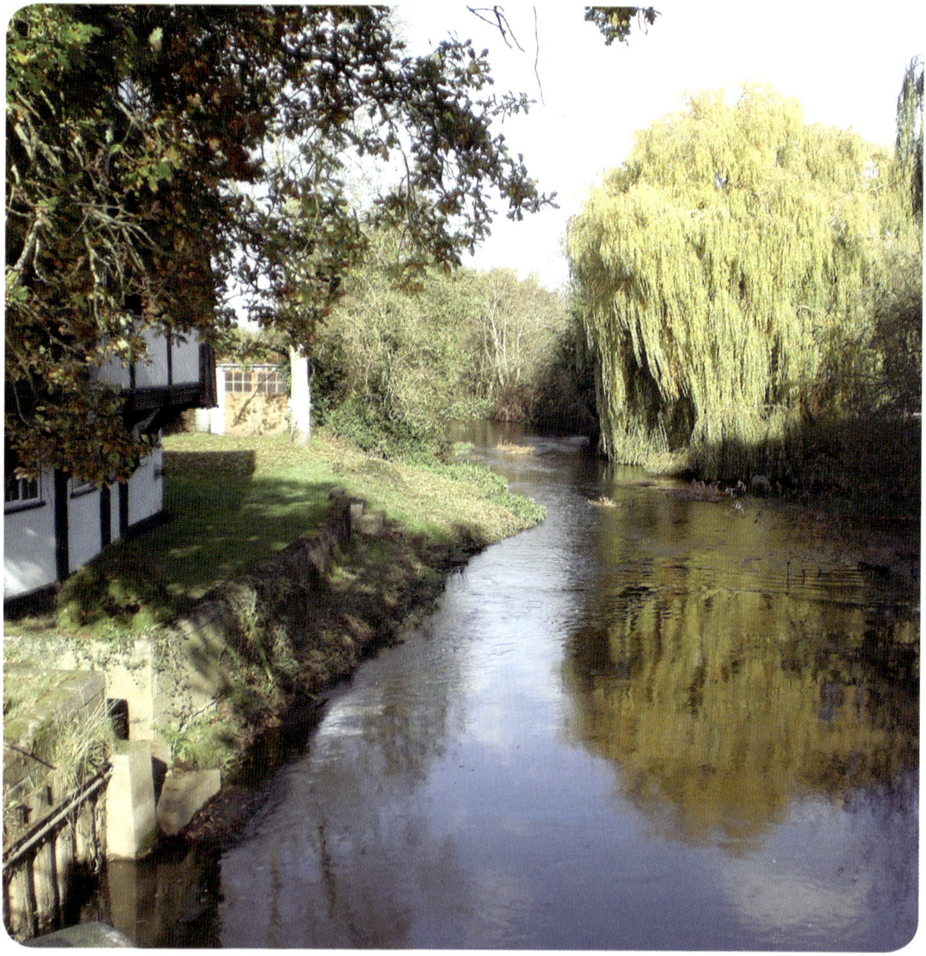

■ *The gentle waters near Twyford.* ■

This is one of those walks that cries out to be tried. With extensive urbanisation just about everywhere you look, genuine unspoilt countryside in this part of east Berkshire is hard to find. However, when, eventually, you get away from the traffic and the constant reminders of modern life, the pleasures of a country walk are greatly appreciated. With the terrain easy and flat, the route is ideally suited to just about everyone in this category. Close to the start are some fine examples of what can be done with former gravel pits – now part of an established nature reserve. On several occasions the walk crosses the path of a busy railway track, one of Isambard Kingdom Brunel's great engineering masterpieces. With his innumerable bridges, viaducts, railway lines and docks, no man did more to change the face of the British landscape than this greatly respected Victorian genius.

GRADE: 2
ESTIMATED CALORIE BURN: 760

Distance: 4½ miles
Stiles: 4
Time: 2 hours
Map: OS Explorer 159 Reading, Wokingham and Pangbourne.
Starting point: The car park in Polehampton Place. GR 786758
How to get there: Take the A4 between Reading and Maidenhead and follow the A3032 for Twyford. Approaching from the west, cross the railway and turn right for the public car park in Polehampton Place. Twyford station is on the Paddington/Reading line.
Refreshments: The Duke of Wellington in Twyford High Street is just a few paces from the car park where the walk starts and is therefore an ideally placed watering hole. Telephone: 0118 934 0456.

1 From the public car park in **Polehampton Place**, walk to the main road and turn left. Cross the railway bridge and then turn left at a footpath sign, following the path through a residential development. Cross **Weavers Way** and keep to the path as it runs beside water. Walk along to a bridge over the **river Loddon** and immediately beyond it turn left. On the right now is the **Loddon Nature Reserve**, the largest group of flooded gravel pits along the Loddon corridor. Continue along the signposted footpath with the river on your left. Lakes can be seen over to the right. Approach railway arches – part of Brunel's railway out of Paddington to the Midlands and West Country – and just before the line you reach a path junction. Keep right here, with the railway on your left through the trees, and follow the path with lakes again visible on the right. Continue to the next waymark and turn left. Pass through the arches and keep ahead on the path to reach a junction with a metalled road.

2 Opposite is a lake. Turn left here and after a few paces join a path running parallel to the road. When the path rejoins the road, cross over to a bridleway on the opposite side and then return to the highway by a rather unusual Alpine-style house with timber cladding. A large willow tree can be seen across the river. Cross the **Loddon** and as the road begins to curve left, turn left to join a bridleway. Follow the broad path between fields and when it swings left, keep straight on along the footpath. On reaching a main road cross over to a signposted byway.

3 Follow the track between trees, fields and hedgerows, disregard a path on the right and with a house visible ahead, look for a path on the left. Cross a field towards woodland, cross a footbridge and turn immediately left, through a tunnel of overhanging branches. Continue to a footbridge and stile, turn right into the field and head towards houses beyond the trees. Pass through a gateway into the next field and keep ahead to a stile leading out to the road. Turn left and follow the road round a bend to a waymarked footpath on the right. Cross two stiles in quick succession and on the right is a good view of **Stanlake Manor**. Go to the next stile and then keep

■ *The Duke of Wellington.* ■

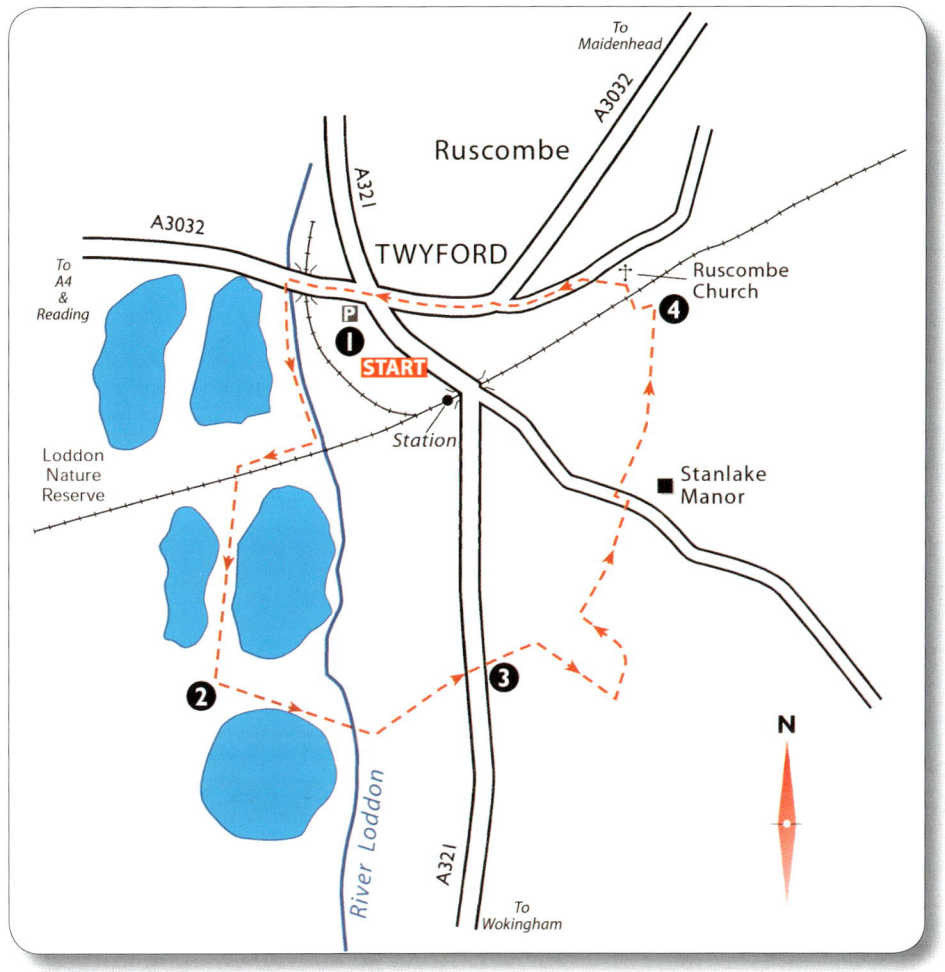

ahead across the next field. Head towards some cottages and turn left at a tarmac lane.

4 Pass a footpath on the right and walk towards **Ruscombe** church tower. Cross the railway, keep left at the church and walk along to the road. Keep left here and follow the highway towards Twyford, avoiding the turning for Bracknell on the left. Follow **Waltham Road** into **Ruscombe Lane** and pass the **Royal Oak** on the right. Keep left at the next main junction and return to the centre of **Twyford**. The **Duke of Wellington pub** is on the left just before **Polehampton Place**.

14 Bracknell
Deep in the Forest

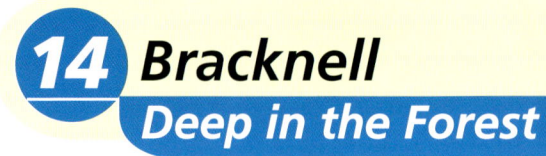

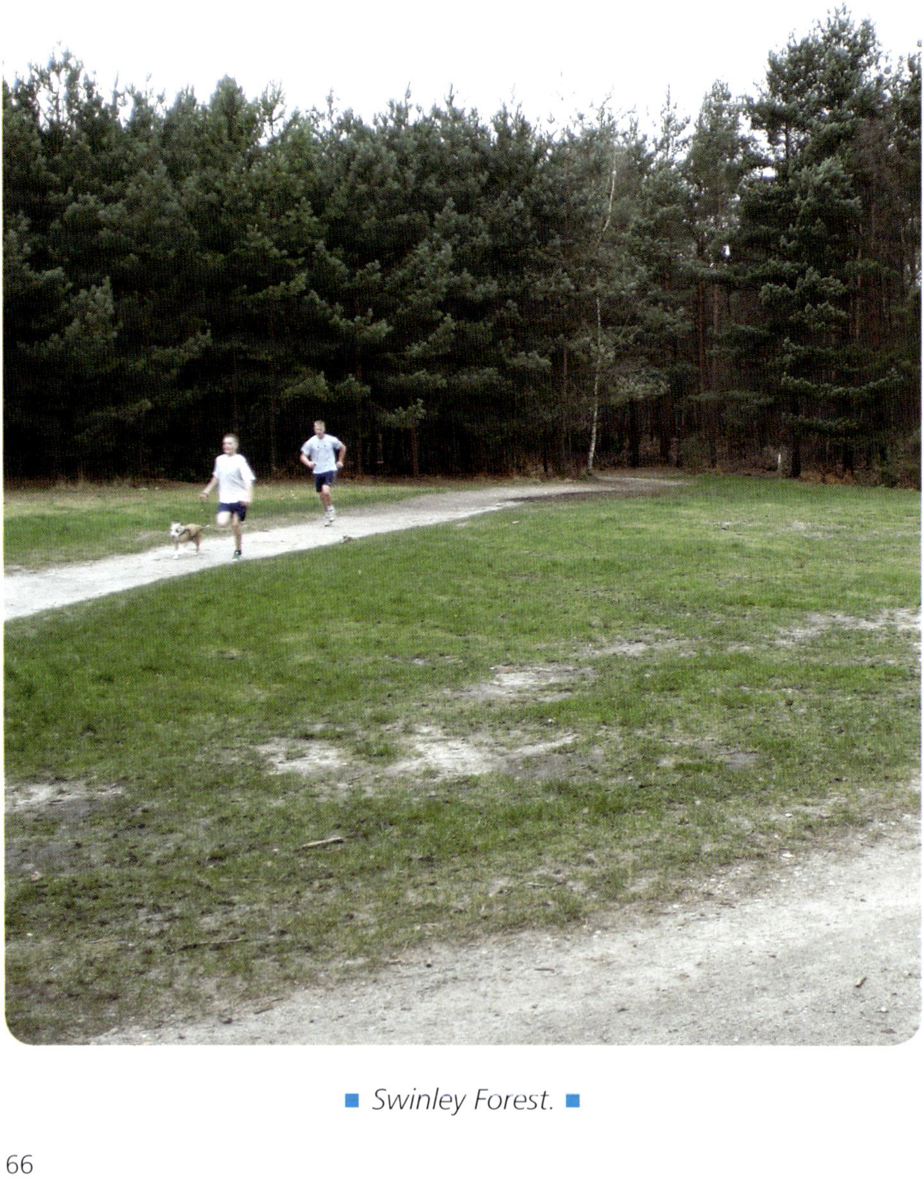

■ *Swinley Forest.* ■

This walk is unique in Berkshire. The terrain is largely easy and level – a mix of paths and tracks – but what sets it apart from the others are the regimented rows of trees stretching as far as the eye can see. You could be forgiven for thinking you are in some sinister forest in one of the old Eastern bloc countries, in a scene perhaps from one of those John le Carré cold war thrillers of the 1960s. Don't worry. You are firmly in Berkshire, only a couple of miles or so from the heart of Bracknell.

The walk starts at the Look Out Discovery Centre, opened in 1991. Come here at the weekend in summer and this country park is thronging. Visit on a weekday in winter and you have the place more or less to yourself. Here, in the largest area of unbroken woodland in Berkshire, you can follow deserted tracks for miles, with only the soothing sigh of the breeze in the pine trees to break the silence. You can make good progress on these clear and obvious trails and you may well be inspired to tackle something a bit longer and more adventurous at the end of this walk.

GRADE: 2
ESTIMATED CALORIE BURN: 560

Distance: 3¼ miles
Stiles: None
Time: 1½ – 2 hours
Map: OS Explorer 160 Windsor, Weybridge and Bracknell.
Starting point: The car park at the Look Out Discovery Centre. GR 876661
How to get there: From Bracknell follow the A322 south to the B3430, turn right and the entrance to the Look Out is on the left. There is plenty of room to park at the Look Out.
Refreshments: The Look Out includes a coffee shop which is open daily and offers hot snacks and a range of drinks. Telephone: 01344 354400.

1 Approach the main entrance to the Look Out building and bear left through a gate leading into a picnic area. Pass a children's playground, go through a gate and at the junction immediately beyond it cross over and follow the **Ramblers Route**, a 26-mile trail skirting Bracknell's town boundaries. Veer left at the next junction, still following the Ramblers Route, and pass a sign for Swinley Forest – 'No horses or cycles'. Go through a gate and soon you begin climbing **Gravel Hill**. The ascent is steep but short. Pass a viewing point on the left and a trig point on the right. Keep ahead on the broad track, following the Ramblers Route deeper and deeper into the

forest. Make for a major intersection, with wooden gates opposite, and go straight over. Continue in the same direction for about 100 yards to the next junction and turn right.

2 Still following the Ramblers Route, pass a turning for the Look Out on the right and keep to the track. At length the outline of **Crowthorne Reservoir** edges into view over to the right. Immediately beyond it you come to another major intersection. Avoid the first right turning and take the second, signposted to the **Devil's Highway**. The route is part of a Roman road which once linked London with Silchester. Keep ahead, following the straight track which runs parallel to a row of power lines. There is a broad grass verge on the left.

3 At the next crossroads turn right onto the **Three Castles Path** which is unmarked at this point. This trail connects the historic castle sites at Winchester, Odiham and Windsor. Avoid turnings to the left and right and keep ahead. Make for another intersection and in front of you is a gate leading out to **Caesar's Camp**, an Iron Age hill fort. Explore this site, reading about its place in history, then turn left out of the gate and follow the track signposted for the Look Out. Pass over a junction to reach a forest pond on the right, then turn left at the junction just beyond it. On a summer's day the sound of children playing at

■ *The Ramblers Route.* ■

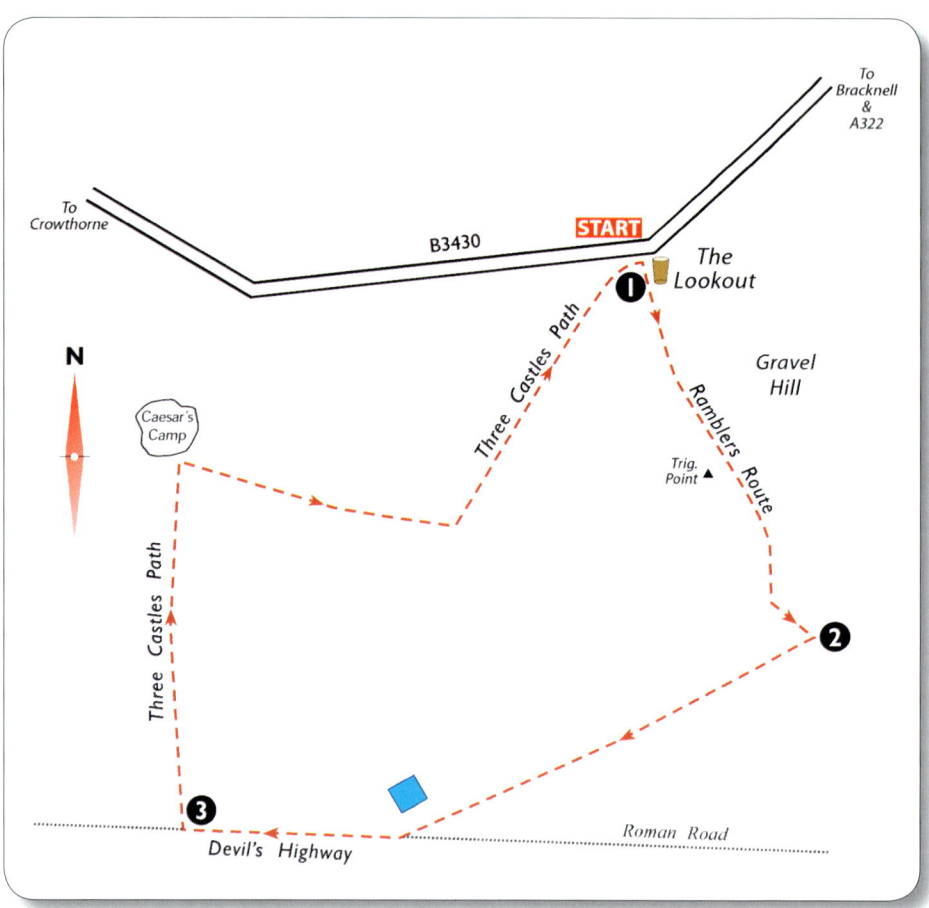

the Look Out is audible on the breeze, a reminder of the contrast between the walk's starting point and its tranquil middle section. On reaching the junction encountered at the beginning of the route, go straight over at the sign for the Look Out and return to the start.

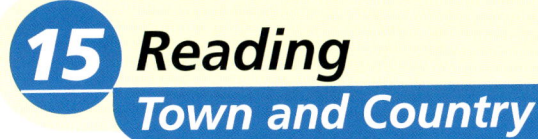

15 Reading

Town and Country

FOOTPATHS FOR FITNESS

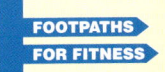

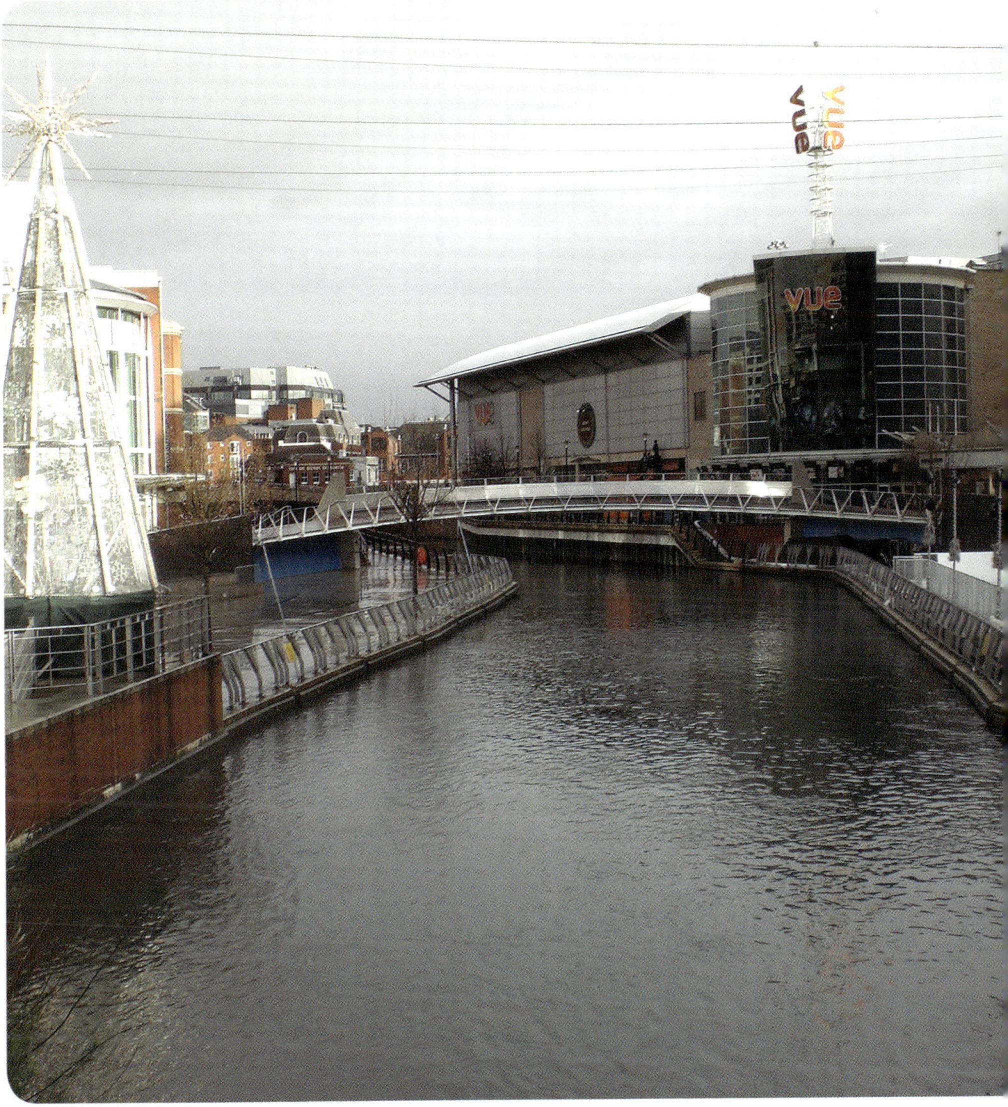

■ *The Kennet and Avon Canal in the centre of Reading.* ■

Again, there are no hills or steep gradients on this medium length walk but it packs a punch nonetheless in terms of variety. You may think you know Reading but do you really know it from a walker's perspective? Maybe not. If you are used to seeing the town from a car or from public transport, then much of this circuit will be new to you. Starting by the Oracle, the walk follows the Kennet and Avon Canal west of Reading to Southcote Mill and then back along the Holy Brook. You start off surrounded by shops and office buildings; within an hour you are following a stretch of the waterway against a leafy, green backdrop. Few decent walks in Berkshire incorporate elements of both town and country.

GRADE: 2
ESTIMATED CALORIE BURN: 820

Distance: 5½ miles
Stiles: None
Time: 2 – 2½ hours
Map: OS Explorer 159 Reading, Wokingham and Pangbourne.
Starting point: The entrance to the Oracle shopping centre by the Kennet and Avon Canal. GR 716733
How to get there: Reading lies off junctions 10, 11 and 12 of the M4. The A4 runs east to west through the town. Reading also has good train services to east and west Berkshire. If coming into the town by car, there are plenty of car parks. Head for the Kennet and Avon Canal waterfront at the Oracle on foot and begin the walk there.
Refreshments: Café Zest, part of House of Fraser, is at the start of the walk, situated in the Oracle shopping centre, right in the heart of Reading. You can relax inside or sit outside overlooking the waterfront. Telephone: 0118 955 7600. The Oracle and Reading town centre offer numerous café bars, pubs and restaurants.

---

1 With Bar Med opposite you, turn right, pass Café Zest and follow the canal towpath to the first of several road bridges. Cross the road by the junction with **Fobney Street** and continue on the towpath. Pass Loch Fyne seafood restaurant and continue beneath the next road bridge. Keep to the towpath at **Temple Place** and walk beneath the next bridge – **Berkeley Avenue**. Across the canal are rows of houses with their gardens running down to the water's edge. Gradually the surroundings become greener and leafier as the Kennet and Avon heads for the countryside to the west of Reading. Keep beside the meandering canal and make for a sign – Bristol 104½ miles,

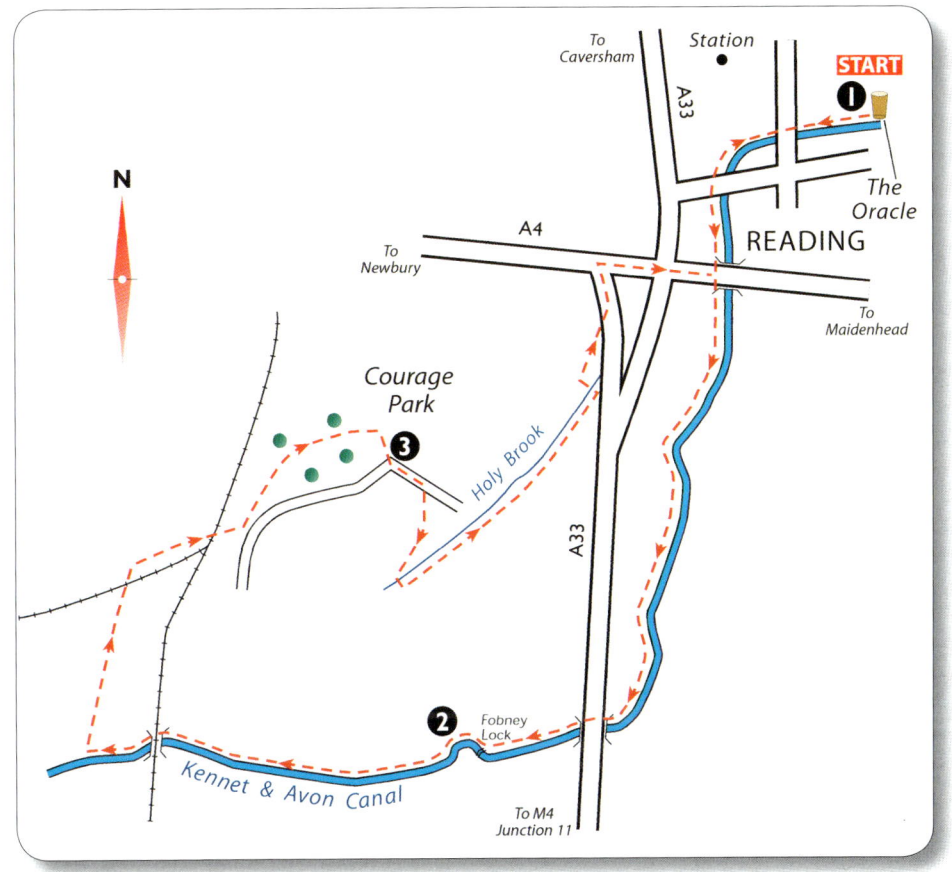

Newbury 18 miles. Follow the towpath towards **Fobney Lock**, cross it and turn right at the sign for Newbury.

2 Begin a lengthy section of straight towpath, with tower blocks at Southcote seen across the fields and meadows. Cross the next weir, turn immediately right and pass under a railway bridge. Cross two footbridges within sight of **Southcote Mill** and then swing right along a track, following it as it curves left. Pass beneath the railway and turn immediately right. Keep fencing on the right and at the next junction turn right, go under the railway again and then turn sharp left. Follow the path along to **Wensley Road**, turn left and walk along to a signposted footpath leading into Courage Park. Follow the main path and beyond the park continue between fencing and houses to a road where there are two lodges.

3 Keep ahead through a kissing gate to rejoin **Wensley Road**, turn right and then left into **Old Lane**. Follow it round to the right at **Brook Mill** and cross the **Holy Brook**. Turn immediately left and follow the bank with houses opposite. Cross the footbridge further on, turn left at a residential development, then right, passing under an arch. At **Rose Kiln Lane** turn left, then right at the lights into **Berkeley Avenue**. Pass above the A33, turn left into **Temple Place** and rejoin the canal towpath, following it back to the **Oracle**.

16 Eton Wick

Trains and Boats and Planes

FOOTPATHS FOR FITNESS

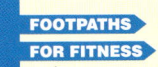

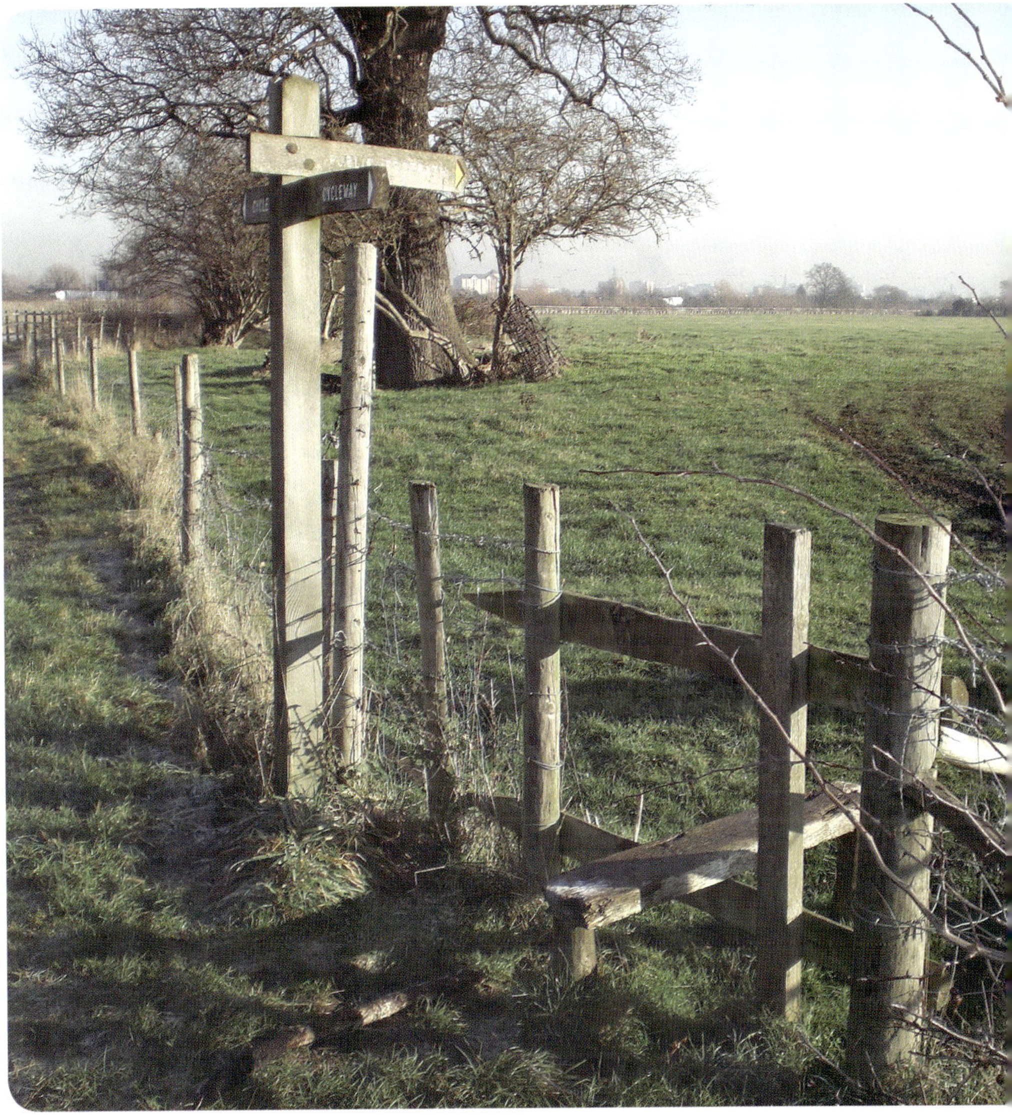

On the path near Eton Wick.

Much of east Berkshire is completely flat and the route of this interesting walk with fine views of Windsor Castle is no exception. Though the scenery is pretty and the surroundings rural, just about every form of transport crops up at some point – there's even a little-known motor museum to visit along the way. There are cars on the busy Windsor relief road, planes landing and taking off at Heathrow, trains clattering along the track between Windsor and Slough, boats on the Thames, cyclists following the path beside the Jubilee river and horses at Windsor races. If you like activity with your walk, then you'll enjoy this one. The hustle and hurly-burly of daily life add to the atmosphere without ruining the magic of the countryside.

The History on Wheels Museum in Eton Wick was established more than 30 years ago and has been described as 'Berkshire's best-kept secret'. Allow an hour or two to walk round the halls and galleries where you'll find a seemingly endless display of vintage motorcycles and military vehicles. Telephone 01753 862637/833833 for times of opening and other information. One of the walk's highlights is the last leg along the Thames. You'll really enjoy this section of the towpath – you can make good headway on this stretch or amble along at a more leisurely pace. Either way, it's great fun. If you have the time and energy, there's also the chance to extend the walk by visiting Eton and Windsor.

GRADE: 2
ESTIMATED CALORIE BURN: 590

Distance: 3½ miles
Stiles: 3
Time: 2 hours
Map: OS Explorer 160 Windsor, Weybridge and Bracknell.
Starting point: Eton Wick Football and Social Club. GR 947785
How to get there: Take the A4 between Slough and Maidenhead and then head south on the B3026 towards Dorney and Eton Wick. On reaching the latter, turn right just beyond the Shepherd's Hut pub and park in the vicinity of Eton Wick Football and Social Club.
Refreshments: The Waterman's Arms is just the place for a simple snack or a hearty meal. While there, glance up at the ceiling and you'll be surprised to see a striking mural depicting the route of the river Thames, complete with many of its most famous features and landmarks. Telephone: 01753 861001.

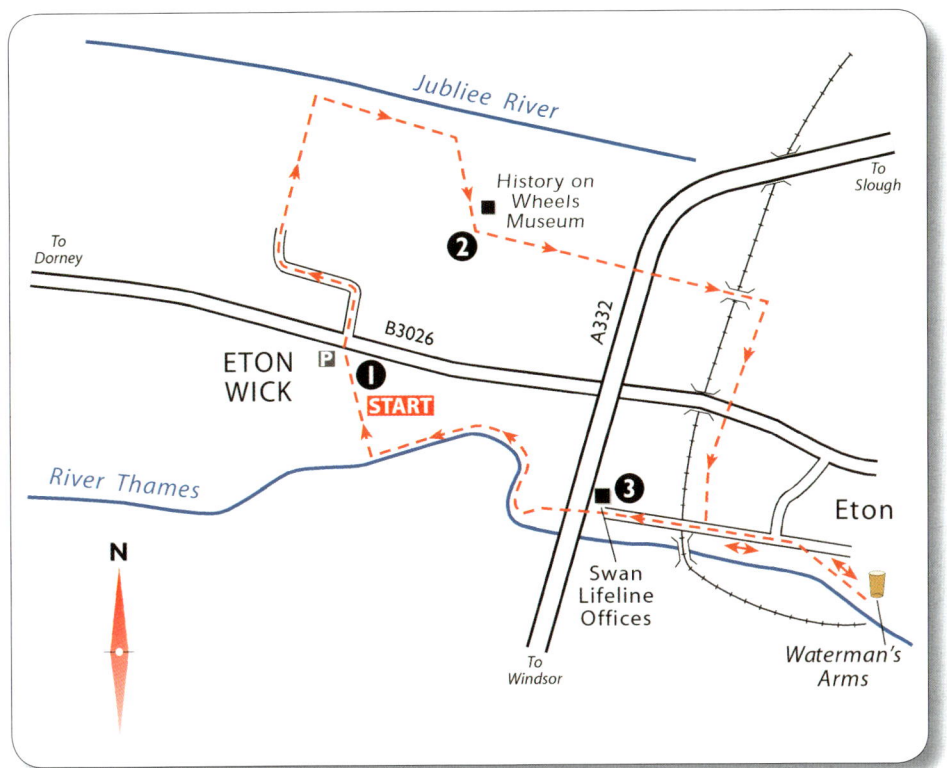

1 Cross the main street into **Bell Lane**. Walk ahead for a short distance, then swing left into **Alma Road**, passing the Primitive Methodist Chapel. Turn right at the next junction on the edge of a green. When the road bends left, go straight on along a bridleway leading to the **Jubilee river**. Turn right immediately before it and follow the waymarked cycle trail to a stile on the right. Cross it to a second stile a few yards ahead and keep along the left edge of the pasture. Avoid a path on the right and make for the field corner by a barn and bungalow. Go slightly right in the next pasture to a stile. On the left here is the entrance to the **History on Wheels Museum**. Keep ahead across several paddocks to reach a track. Turn right and when it bends right, go straight on alongside fencing.

2 Approaching a stile, turn left in front of it and follow the track, passing beneath the Eton relief road. Swing left, then bend right to follow a track between fields. Pass under the railway bridge and turn immediately right. Keep the arches on your right, follow the tarmac path and turn left for 50 yards on reaching the road. Cross over and follow the cycle path, still with the railway arches visible on the right. There is an excellent view from here of Windsor Castle's magnificent Round Tower standing proud above the town. On reaching a lane you have a choice.

To visit Eton and Windsor where there are refreshments, turn left and walk along to the next road junction. Veer right here and head diagonally across the meadows towards the river. Walk towards Eton and ahead is the **Waterman's Arms**, the first of many pubs and inns in the village. Adjacent Windsor has an even greater choice of pubs, coffee shops and restaurants. *Retrace your steps* across the meadows to the road, turn left and walk along to the entrance to the Swan Lifeline offices.

3 Keep ahead on the track between trees and when you reach a T-junction turn left to follow a signposted path. Head for the **Thames Path**, turn left for a few paces to look at **Cuckoo Weir** and the Chinese Bridge – a rather picturesque spot on the river. Return to the main walk and follow the riverbank with the Thames on your left. Windsor racecourse is clearly visible on the opposite bank. Pass a memorial stone dedicated to the memory of John Lionel Baker, a brilliant swimmer who spent much of his time on this stretch of the river. Read the rather amusing bathing regulations on the reverse side of the stone. Continue towards a footbridge and turn right just before it towards **Eton Wick**. On reaching an intersection, with a bridge on the left, keep straight on. Make for a sports field and keep on the tarmac path running along its right-hand perimeter. Turn left at the T-junction and return to the car park where the walk began.

■ *Windsor's famous railway arches.* ■

17 Theale
Ratty and Mole Were Here!

FOOTPATH
FOR FITNE

■ *Showing the way at Sulham.* ■

This straightforward, medium-length walk explores a little-known pocket of tranquil countryside just to the west of Reading. Starting in the village of Theale, renowned for its vast church, the route runs through the hamlet of North Street, sandwiched between the M4 and the A340. Not far from the main route lies Moor Copse Nature Reserve and also the river Pang. According to some sources, this stretch of the river was a favourite haunt of author Kenneth Grahame who lived in Berkshire and wrote what became a children's classic *The Wind in the Willows* in 1908. Beyond Sulham church you can speed things up a bit and set a cracking pace along a lengthy section of track cutting through farmland at the heart of the countryside.

GRADE: 2
ESTIMATED CALORIE BURN: 900

Distance: 5¾ or 4½ miles
Stiles: 5
Time: 2½ hours
Map: OS Explorer 159 Reading, Wokingham and Pangbourne.
Starting point: Theale High Street. GR 644714
How to get there: Theale lies just to the west of Reading, close to junction 12 of the M4. There is also a railway station nearby.
Refreshments: La Baguetterie in Theale High Street is a stylish coffee shop offering a range of snacks and cakes. Telephone 0118 930 2444. For a summer's evening, you may wish to choose one of Theale's many pubs and inns for a drink and something to eat after the walk.

---

1 From the **High Street** head west to **Englefield Road** on the right. Take the road, look for a Catholic church and take the next waymarked path on the right. Follow the path to the next road by some bungalows and turn left. Pass through an alleyway to the next road and then go straight across the green into **North Walk**. Keep to the left of some lock-up garages and follow an enclosed path running north. Walk along to the entrance to a golf club and continue on the path, avoiding a footpath with a galvanised kissing gate on the right. Turn right at the road and follow it through **North Street**.

2 When the road bends sharp left, go straight on along a no through road, following it round to the right at the next junction. Keep to the tarmac lane, signposted as a footpath, and ignore a path on the right. Walk along

■ *Sulham church.* ■

to **Pond Farm** and continue ahead at the galvanised gate. Pass alongside dilapidated farm outbuildings and ahead of you now is an M4 footbridge. Climb it and descend into a secluded wood. Cross another footbridge – albeit much smaller and more basic – and follow the broad grassy ride between plantations. Before long you come to a junction with a track. *If you wish to shorten the walk*, go straight on here, turn right at the next track and follow it back to **Theale**. *To complete the full walk*, turn left and skirt the field edge to its corner. Cross a style and turn left to a footbridge and a path leading to **Moor Copse Nature Reserve**. If you wish to visit the nature reserve, turn left down the path. To continue the walk, turn left and continue along the perimeter to the next stile. In the next field an old wartime pillbox can be seen on the right. Head diagonally across the pasture to a double stile and footbridge, then cross the next field to a stile leading out to the road.

3 Turn right and continue for about 70 yards to a track on the right. Take the track – **Nunhide Lane** – pass **Sulham church** and at length you come to **Coltmoor Cottages** on the right. Keep ahead to **Nunhide Farm** and remain on the track as it passes close to the motorway. On reaching a junction, walk a few steps towards retail outlets and business units and turn sharp right to cross the M4 at the footbridge. Follow the road back into the centre of **Theale**.

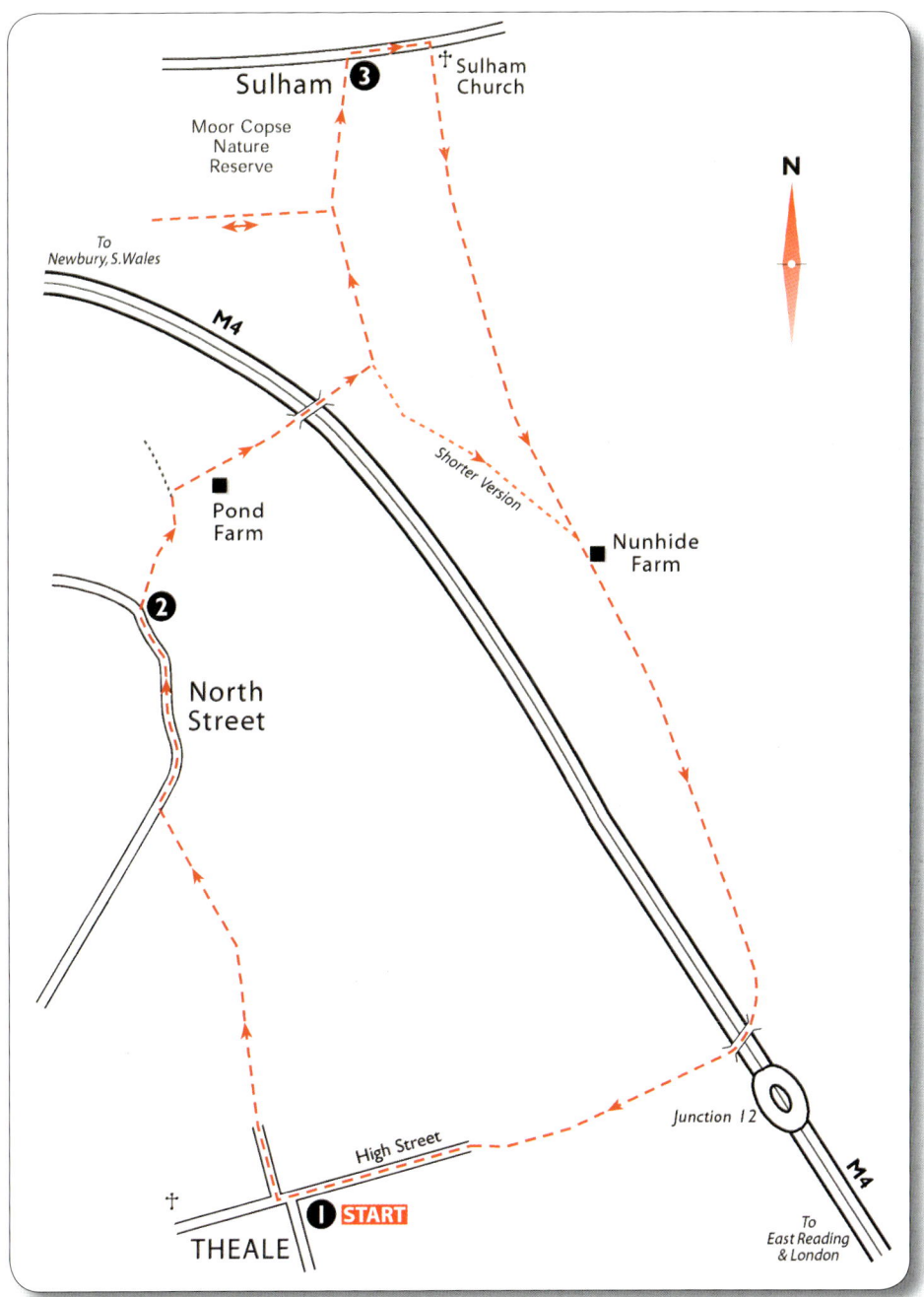

Sulham

❸

† Sulham Church

Moor Copse Nature Reserve

To Newbury, S.Wales

M4

Pond Farm

❷

Shorter Version

Nunhide Farm

North Street

Junction 12

M4

High Street

❶ START

† THEALE

To East Reading & London

N

18 Hungerford

Setting a Good Pace

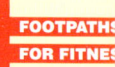

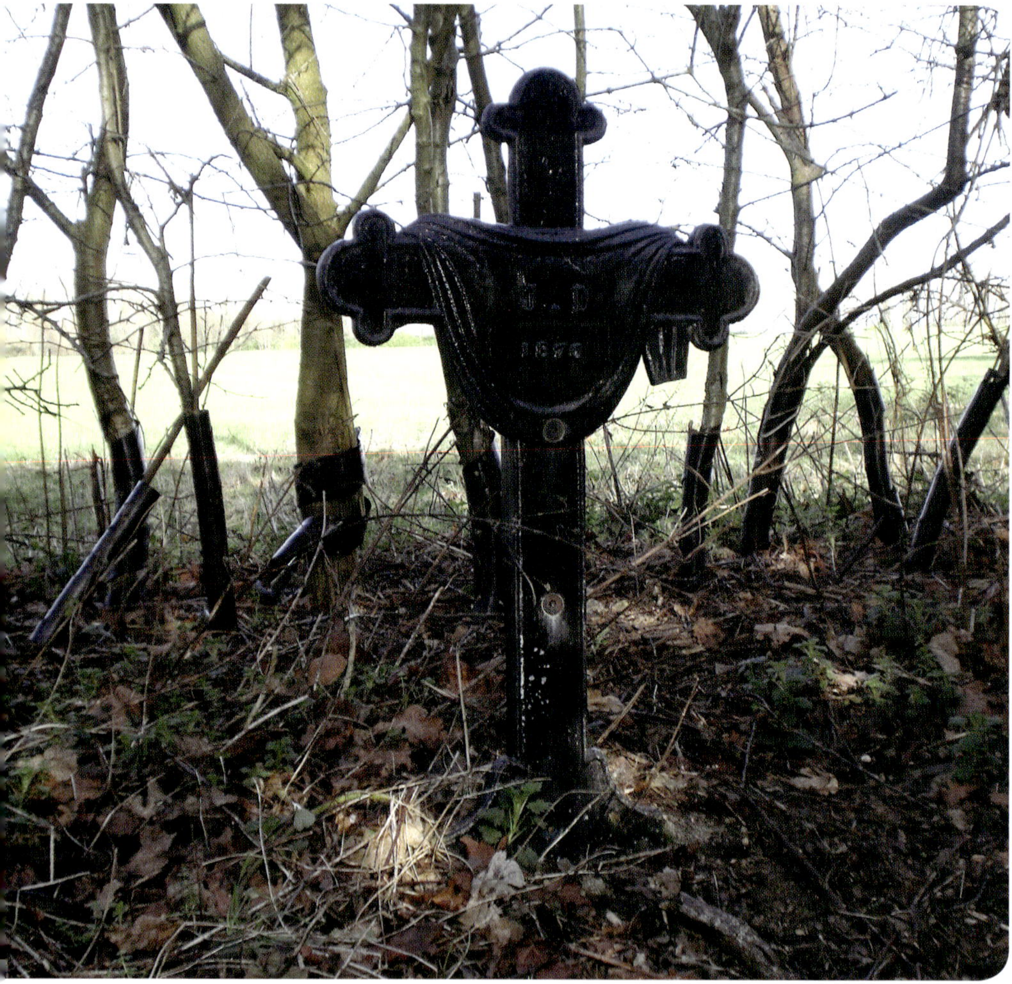

The memorial to a 19th-century murder victim.

To the north of Hungerford lies a peaceful corner of rural Berkshire that, surprisingly, is often overlooked by both casual strollers and more earnest walkers. Here, gently undulating downland and farmland stretch to the horizon and the only sound is the distant hum of traffic on the M4 motorway. About 100 years before the motorway was built, this tranquil pocket of countryside was even quieter. Nothing much happened in these parts – except, that is, for the night of 11 December 1876, when two local policemen, Inspector Joseph Drewitt and PC Thomas Shorter, came across a group of poachers and were brutally murdered. The killers were later caught and sentenced to death. Two memorials, close to the route of the walk, mark the scene of the crime. There is some gentle climbing on the route but on the whole the walk is over level farmland and along quiet country lanes. Beyond the Tally-Ho pub, you follow farmland tracks which are perfect for testing and improving your walking skills. Set a good pace and see how you fare at the end of this stretch.

GRADE: 3
ESTIMATED CALORIE BURN: 1140

Distance: 7 miles
Stiles: 6
Time: 3 hours
Map: OS Explorer 158 Newbury and Hungerford.
Starting point: Hungerford station. GR 341685
How to get there: Hungerford is about 8 miles west of Newbury. Follow the A4 and on reaching the town, turn off by the Bear Hotel. Head up the High Street, turn left into Park Street and the turning to the station is on the left. Hungerford is served by regular train services from Newbury and Reading.
Refreshments: The Tutti Pole is a traditional family-run tearoom at the bottom end of the High Street, close to the Kennet and Avon Canal. Telephone: 01488 682515. Alternatively, there are a number of pubs in and around Hungerford and one midway round the route.

1 From the station, cross the line and the **Kennet and Avon Canal** and follow the obvious path to the **John O'Gaunt** pub. Turn right, then right at the next junction, cross the Kennet and then swing left at the 'Eddington - village only' sign. Follow the riverbank path to a lane on a bend. Continue on the path to reach a tarmac drive leading to a bungalow. Walk ahead for a few steps and go straight on when the drive swings right. Follow the path parallel to the road and when you eventually merge with it at a junction, go straight on. Pass **New Hayward Farm** on the left and take the next right-hand path.

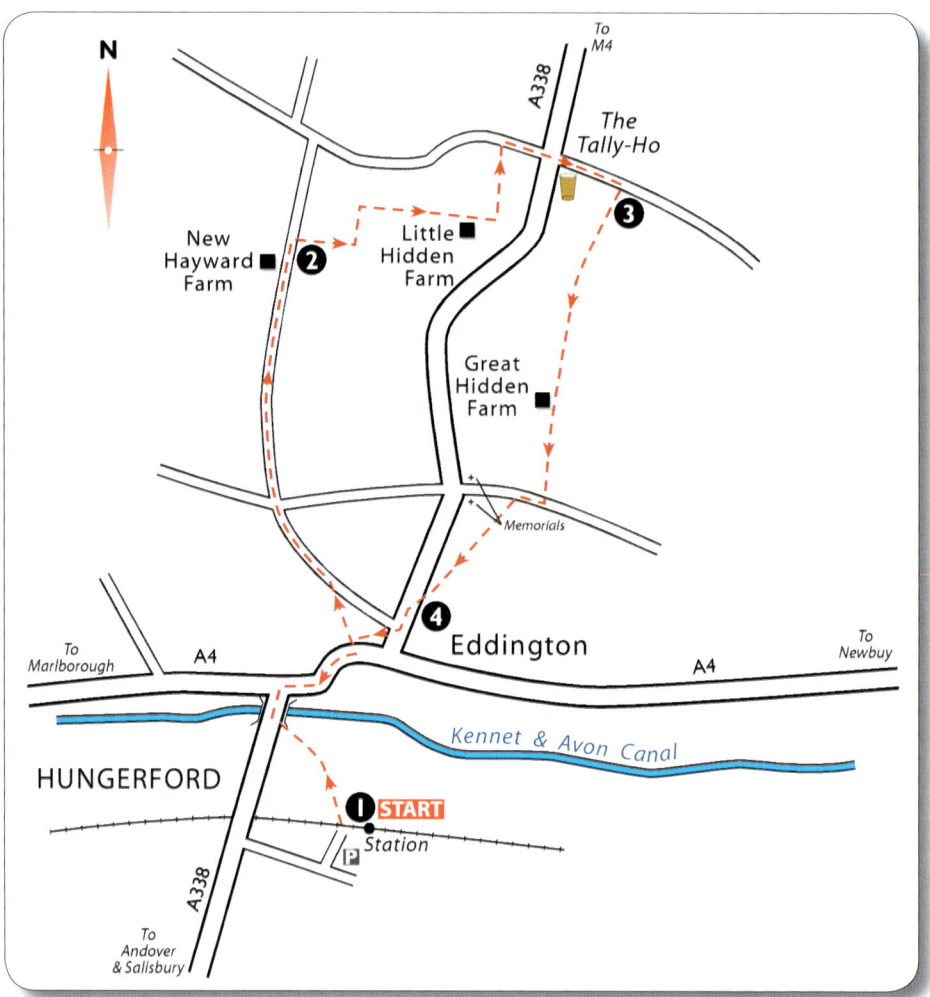

2 Go round the left edge of the field to a gate by trees. Turn left down the field edge, making for a stile in the corner. Cross it and turn right, keeping to the left of woodland. Follow the field to the far corner, go through the gate and take the track ahead. When it swings right towards **Little Hidden Farm**, go straight along a grassy path between trees. Bear right and skirt the outbuildings to reach the main access track. Turn left, then left again to join a path leading to the road. Turn right to the A338 and go straight across by the **Tally-Ho pub**. Pass a footpath on the left and then swing right just a few paces beyond it.

3 Avoid the track; instead keep to the right of it, heading up the field slope with trees and hedgerow on the left. Avoid a path to the right and continue heading south. Keep to the left of **Great Hidden Farm**, cross a cattle grid and briefly follow the drive. After 60 yards turn right at a hidden waymark and follow the grassy path to the field corner. Go out to the road and turn right for the junction with the A338. On the right is a memorial inscribed with the initials JD - (Joseph Drewitt). To the left, on the main road, is the second memorial to TS - (Thomas Shorter). Turn around and go back down the lane and take the path on the right. Head diagonally across the pasture, keeping to the left of some trees. Look for a stile and cross into the next field. Head diagonally left and make for the far corner. Cross a stile into woodland and look for a second stile giving access to a small pasture. Go right to a pair of stiles leading onto the A338.

4 Turn left and walk along to the entrance to the cemetery, then right about 70 yards before the A4 to reach the Kennet. From here retrace your steps back to **Hungerford** town centre.

■ *The River Kennet.* ■

19 Greenham

A Common Reclaimed

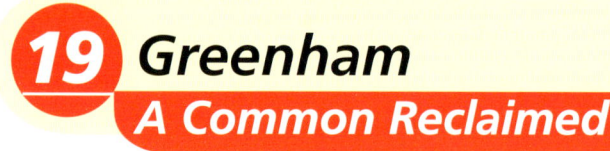

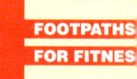

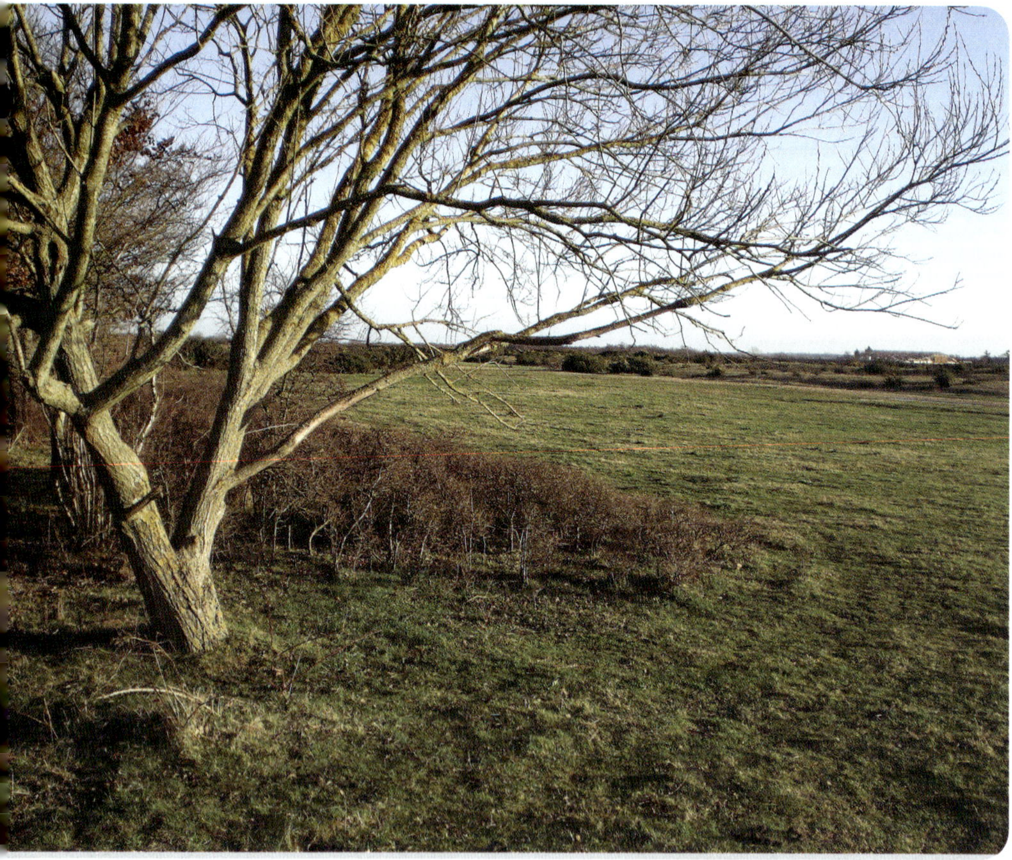

■ *The breezy expanses of Greenham Common.* ■

You'll probably need to summon a little extra puff when you climb out of the Kennet valley onto Crookham Common and Greenham Common, but other than that, this is a walk which, apart from its length, offers little to tax those of average fitness. The circuit begins at the Thatcham Nature Discovery Centre. The lakes here were once part of a series of pits excavated for gravel in the 1970s and subsequently reclaimed for wildlife in the 1980s. Back then, hardly a day seemed to go by when the American air base at Greenham Common didn't feature on television news bulletins. CND rallies, candlelit vigils, women's peace marches and attempts to cut the 9-mile security fencing highlighted the presence of 96 nuclear-armed cruise missiles at Greenham. The military left long ago and today Greenham is a very different place, with broad and breezy paths and tracks replacing the runways and other unsightly reminders of the cold war. The great thing about walking here is the wonderful sense of space and distance the old airfield conveys. It's just the place to attempt a bit of a spurt and work up some steam. The walk starts and finishes with a very pleasant leafy stretch of the Kennet and Avon Canal, one of the south's best-known inland waterways, built almost 200 years ago.

GRADE: 3
ESTIMATED CALORIE BURN: 1330

Distance: 8½ or 6 miles
Stiles: None
Time: 4 hours
Map: OS Explorer 158 Newbury and Hungerford.
Starting point: Thatcham Nature Discovery Centre. GR 506671
How to get there: Follow Lower Way which runs parallel to, and south of, the A4 between Thatcham and Newbury. The entrance to the Thatcham Nature Discovery Centre is clearly marked and there is plenty of room to park. Thatcham station is on the Newbury/Reading/ Paddington line and you may wish to travel by train and begin the walk there.
Refreshments: The Swan by Thatcham station is a good pub for snacks and main meals. Telephone: 01635 862084. Coffee and light snacks are available at the Discovery Centre. Telephone: 01635 874381.

1 From the door of the **Discovery Centre** turn left and follow the lakeside path, keeping the water on your left. When the path ultimately sweeps left, go straight on, heading south on a signposted path. Cross the railway line and follow the clear path beside lakes and reed beds. On reaching the towpath of the **Kennet and Avon Canal**, turn left and pass turf-sided **Widmead Lock**. Keep ahead on the towpath towards Thatcham station and at length you reach a bridleway crossing the canal.

To shorten the walk turn right here and follow the track uphill to the road. Head west across **Greenham Common** to the control tower car park.

To complete the full walk, keep ahead along the Kennet and Avon

■ *Looking south across Greenham Common.* ■

towpath to the next road bridge by Thatcham station, leave the waterway here and turn right. Swing left into **Chamberhouse Mill Lane**, pass the mill and follow a gravel drive. When it bends left by a house called Crookham Willows, go straight on along the bridleway. Head uphill into trees and when you reach the higher ground, turn right about 100 yards before the main road. Follow the path across a track, pass a small reservoir on the left and at the next intersection turn left to follow a tarmac track running through the woods.

2 On reaching **Crookham Common Road** on a bend, cross over and turn right to reach a parking area. Follow the lane ahead and then continue across **Crookham Common**, keeping right at a fork. After some time the disused control tower edges into view. Keep right at a fork where an old white flagpost is seen. Turn right just beyond it and keep the post on your right. Look for a pond with the road beyond. On reaching a building numbered 309, swing left towards a warehouse. Turn sharp right after about 100 yards and follow a broad waymarked path. As you approach the warehouse, at the point where the path curves left, turn sharp right, avoid a gate, and keep along the left-hand hedge to a gate leading out to the road.

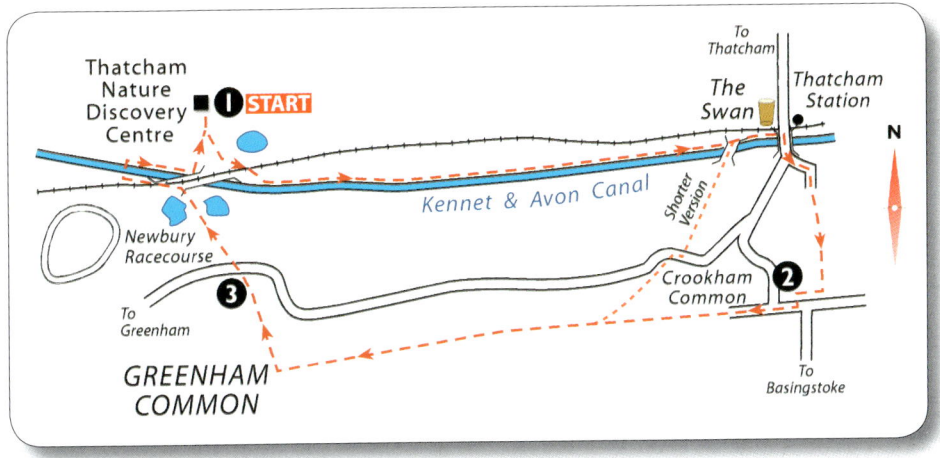

3 Cross over and follow the track beside **Bowdown Nature Reserve**. Walk beside a golf course and then alongside Newbury racecourse. Pass under the railway, then turn right at a swing bridge and right again at the towpath. Pass a lock, cross a wooden footbridge and then turn sharp left. Keep right at the fork, cross a footbridge and turn right. On reaching a track, keep left and when you come to the corner of the lake, rejoin the path at the start of the walk.

■ *The lake at Thatcham Discovery Centre.* ■

■ *The Long Walk.* ■

At the heart of east Berkshire lies a unique landscape perfectly suited to walkers of all ages. Windsor Great Park is a walker's paradise, a vast outdoor playground where the novice stroller and the hardened hiker can escape the hustle and bustle of 21st-century life and indulge their favourite pastime. This is where those new to walking can practise and improve their skills and those with years of experience under their belts can easily complete the day's jaunt.

Beginning at Bishopsgate, one of the entrances to the park, the walk makes for the Copper Horse statue and then heads off for Virginia Water, Smith's Lawn – the renowned polo ground – and finally the Savill Gardens where you may succumb to a cup of tea and a light snack before finishing the walk. Windsor Great Park is one of those places that lures you back time and again. This is a fascinating corner of Berkshire – a place of infinite beauty and great character, a bustling community and a working environment.

GRADE: 3
ESTIMATED CALORIE BURN: 1260

Distance: 8 miles
Stiles: None
Time: 4 hours
Map: OS Explorer 160 Windsor, Weybridge and Bracknell.
Starting point: The car park near the Fox and Hounds pub on Bishopsgate Road. GR 987722
How to get there: From the A30, to the south of Windsor Great Park, follow the signs for Englefield Green, pass the expansive green and then turn left into Bishopsgate Road. There are parking spaces as you approach the entrance to Windsor Great Park. From the north follow the A308 towards Staines and turn off for Englefield Green. After about 1 mile turn right into Castle Hill Road, then right at the next junction into Bishopsgate Road.
Refreshments: The Fox and Hounds pub is a popular pub right next door to Windsor Great Park. Especially popular at weekends, the inn offers a good range of snacks and more substantial fare. Telephone 01784 433098. The café at Savill Gardens is a perfect choice in summer with indoor and outdoor seating and the chance to relax after the rigours of the walk.

1 From the parking area near the **Fox and Hounds** walk down to **Bishopsgate**. Pass **Bishopsgate Lodge** and continue down the drive in the direction

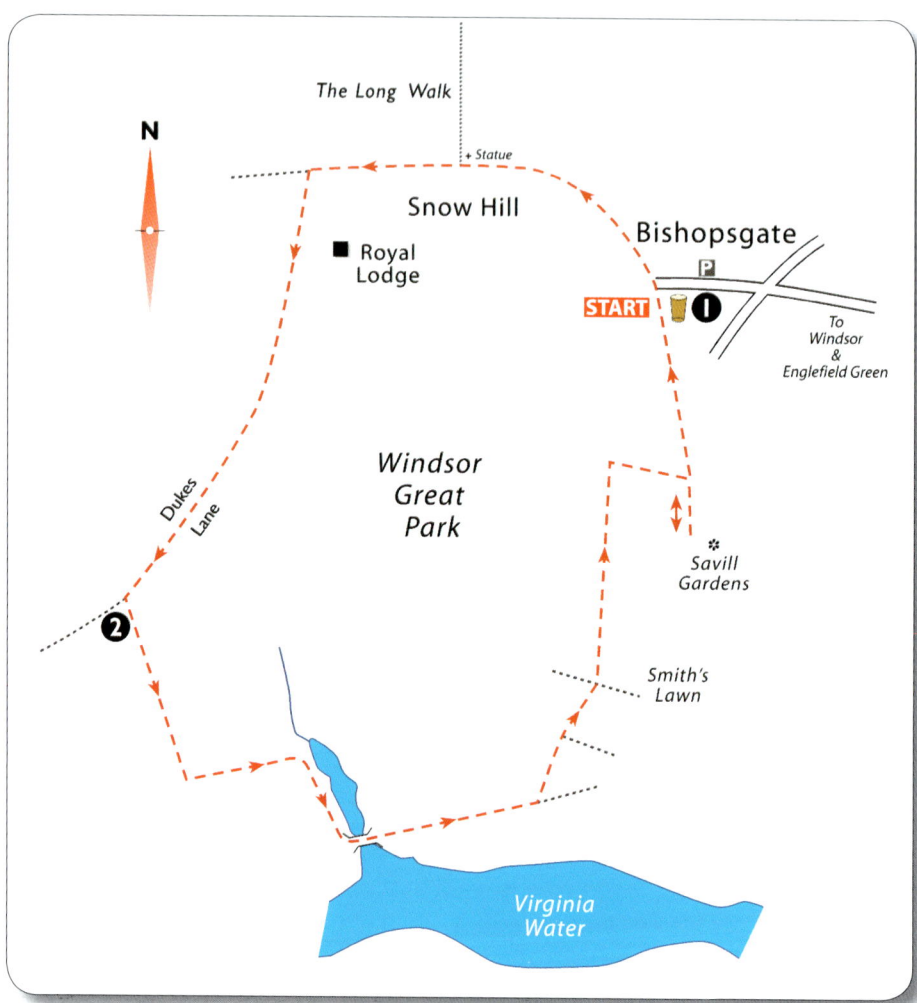

The Long Walk

N

+ Statue

Snow Hill

■ Royal Lodge

Bishopsgate

P

START 🍺 ❶

To Windsor & Englefield Green

Windsor Great Park

Dukes Lane

❷

❀ Savill Gardens

Smith's Lawn

Virginia Water

of **Royal Lodge**. At the next junction, before reaching the gatehouses, turn right and pass between a deer fence and a security fence. **Windsor Castle** looms into view on the horizon. Keep ahead, crossing over the **Long Walk**. Snow Hill, at its southern end, is crowned by the famous equestrian statue of George III, known as the Copper Horse. From this point there is a magnificent view down the Long Walk to Windsor Castle. Continue down the drive to the next security gate, veer immediately left and soon **Royal Lodge**, the former home of the Queen Mother, is seen over to the left. Go straight on at the next intersection and keep ahead at the next junction along **Duke's Lane**. Follow it for some distance, pass a private road on the left, drop down the hill and curve to the right. As you begin to climb towards some houses, look for a track on the right with a 'private area' sign.

2 Turn left opposite it to join a woodland riding track. Follow it for some distance and ultimately you veer half left onto a path with a sign saying 'No entry for horses,' following it alongside the tree-fringed **Virginia Water**. On reaching a road, turn left over the bridge and follow the parallel path. Pass houses and keep going beside the road. Cross the next bridge and pass signs for Valley Gardens. Head towards **Smith's Lawn** and, on reaching it, continue ahead alongside this world-famous polo ground for about 1 mile. Turn right immediately before a lodge by a sign 'Access to the Savill Gardens'. When the lane bends right, you have a choice. Continue ahead to visit the gardens; otherwise turn left here and the follow the broad path back to **Bishopsgate** where the walk began.

Calorie Chart

The following chart shows the approximate calories spent per hour by a person weighing 8 stone (112 lbs), 17 stone (238 lbs) and 20 stone (280 lbs)

	8 stone	17 stone	20 stone
Walking, 2 mph	160	240	312
Walking, 3 mph	210	320	416
Walking, 4½ mph	295	440	572

Note that these figures are based on moderate, not vigorous, activity.